The Christian Scholar in the Age of the Reformation

E. Harris Harbison

William B. Eerdmans Publishing Company
Grand Rapids, Michigan

Library of Congress Cataloging in Publication Data

Harbison, E. Harris (Elmore Harris), 1907-1964.
The Christian scholar in the age of the Reformation.

Reprint. Originally published: New York : Scribner,
1956.
1. Learning and scholarship.   2. Reformation.
I. Title.
AZ346.H37   1983   001   83-16511
ISBN 0-8028-1975-3 (pbk.)

Preface

THIS brief book is based on five lectures delivered on the L. P. Stone Foundation at Princeton Theological Seminary during April 1955. It seemed appropriate for a layman and a historian speaking before such an audience to choose some subject which lay at the crossroads of his interests and his hearers'. It occurred to me that scholarship as a Christian calling was a subject relatively neglected by both historians and theologians and that it was worth inquiring into. Rather than to celebrate Christian scholars in general, it seemed best to focus upon the Reformation, both because it was the period I knew best and because the Protestant Reformers were the source of the tradition of a learned ministry which had produced Princeton Seminary. So what follows is an attempt to suggest what a Christian scholar is like, how he comes by a sense of his calling, how he may reconcile his scholarly zeal with his Christian faith, and how his work affects the development of Christianity, through a study of a few Christian scholars of the Reformation period and some of their predecessors who influenced them.

The method followed is to talk in particular rather than in general, to concentrate on a few important and well-known figures rather than to catalogue the many, to suggest rather than to conclude. A thorough study of the subject, of course, should go much further. It should ask what happened in general to Christian scholarship between the decline of scholasticism and the beginnings of modern science. It should examine and describe dozens, if not hundreds, of Christian scholars. It should relate the new doubts and concerns and conclusions of these scholars to the changing social conditions and revolutionary movements of their day. The purpose of the present essay is far more modest. It is to suggest a somewhat fresh perspective from which the familiar outlines of the age of the Reformation may be viewed.

This perspective may be described briefly as follows. The Protestant Reformation began in a scholar's insight into the meaning of Scripture. It was to a large extent a learned movement, a thing of professors and students, a scholars' revolution, as later chapters will suggest. The Catholic response to the challenge, particularly in the Council of Trent, partook of the same nature. The prestige and influence of Christian scholars probably never stood higher in all of Western history than during the two generations which embraced the lifetimes of Erasmus, Luther, and Calvin. In no other period is there anything quite like the zest for learning, the respect for scholarship, the confidence in what scholarship might accomplish—and the revolution it did accomplish—of the age of the Reformation. It was Christian scholars over and over again who made the sixteenth-century equivalent of the headlines, and it is they who still crowd the statesmen in the indexes of our textbooks on the period: Tyndale, Cranmer, and Hooker from England, for example; Budé and Lefèvre from France; Reuchlin and Mutian in Germany; Contarini and Valdes in Italy; Ximénez and Vives from Spain. There were scholarly Popes, and Reginald Pole was by no means the only scholar in the College of Cardinals. On all sides of the complex religious controversy, leader after leader could be described as a "scholar" in some sense of the word. Sir Thomas More was a statesman with the instincts and equipment of a scholar. Philip Melanchthon was a university professor, as was John Eck. Zwingli and Bucer were writers and teachers as well as preachers. And among the radicals, Sebastian Franck, Conrad Grebel, Sebastian Castellio, and Michael Servetus were only a few of those who could be called scholars. Christian scholars have probably never been so squarely in the historical limelight before or since.

The psychological and spiritual tensions within these learned Christians are particularly interesting to study during the years when men had lost faith in the scholastic method but as yet knew nothing of "science" in the modern sense. During this interim the interests of scholars in general turned from what we would call philosophy and logic to philology and history. The question was what if anything had these disciplines to do with Christian faith? Only a few scholars of the time were significantly disturbed by this problem and became articulate about it. Many of them had no real personal concern with Christianity as a religion. Many of the great Christians of the age had no interest in scholarship. Some who were both practising Christians and scholars left us so few records that it is fruitless to inquire whether they had a sense of vocation or how they acquired it. A few, however, gained a distinct and sometimes hard-won consciousness of calling as scholars, as Christian men of learning, and it is with these that we shall be mainly concerned: with John Colet, who opened new horizons in his lectures at Oxford on St. Paul; Erasmus, who gave his life to "serving God by advancing knowledge" (in P. S. Allen's memorable phrase); Martin Luther, who was Professor of Bible throughout his public career and an indefatigable biblical scholar and translator; and John Calvin, who always thought of himself as first of all a scholar. There is no better age than the Reformation in which to study the Christian scholar and his *vocatio*, in the traditionally ambiguous sense of the word as both divine calling and professional occupation. If modern publishers were as favorable to lengthy titles as their sixteenth-century brethren, this book would be called "The Christian Scholar and His Calling in the Age of the Reformation."

It is a pleasure to acknowledge that this disquisition about scholars rests squarely upon the scholarship of many others, all the way from the sixteenth century to the twentieth. The footnotes will suggest my debt to the standard works of editing and research in the field. Special mention should be made of one work which reached me after my manuscript was in the hands of the publisher: W. Schwarz, *Principles and Problems of Biblical Translation: Some Reformation Controversies and Their Background,* Cambridge University Press, 1955. Had it appeared earlier, my debt to it would have been larger than it has been. I am grateful to the Faculty of Princeton Theological Seminary for the invitation to deliver the Stone Lectures, and to Princeton University for the semester's leave of absence and the research assistance which enabled me to commit them to paper. I am also grateful to the University of Southern California for the invitation to deliver three Arensberg Lectures on this theme in April 1956. My colleagues, Professors Joseph R. Strayer and Whitney J. Oates, have generously read the manuscript as has also Professor Roland H. Bainton of Yale University. Their help has been invaluable. Friends at Princeton Seminary, particularly Professor Bruce M. Metzger, Professor Georges A. Barrois, and Dr. Walter G. Hards, have also been generous with suggestions. My student, Bennett D. Hill, has helped me indefatigably with numerous details. Miss Elizabeth D'Arcy, Mrs. Eileen Blumenthal, and Mrs. Louis E. Gantz have typed the manuscript in various stages.

To my wife, whose quick understanding and constant encouragement have meant more to a diffident author than even she will ever know, the book is dedicated.

E. H. H.

Princeton, N. J.
August 1956

Contents

xi

Scholarship as a Christian Calling

From Jerome to Aquinas

THE Christian scholar—like the Christian poet, the Christian musician, or the Christian scientist—has always run the risk of being dismissed as an anomaly. What has learning to do with salvation of the soul, or satisfaction of the mind with peace of the spirit? "What has Athens to do with Jerusalem, the Academy with the Church?" Tertullian asked in the third century. "What is there in common between the philosopher and the Christian, the pupil of Hellas and the pupil of Heaven?" His own answer was flat enough: "We have no need for curiosity since Jesus Christ, nor for inquiry since the Evangel." [1] Yet the fact is that almost from the beginning of Christianity there have been those who pursued learning as a Christian calling, in the belief that they were following God's will. These followers of an apparently anomalous vocation have never re-

---

[1] *De praescriptione haereticorum*, 7, and *Apologeticus*, 46, in C. N.

ceived the attention they perhaps deserve. In fact, it can be argued that justice has never been done to the scholar as a Christian type, over against the saint, the prophet, and the priest. We hear much of St. Thomas Aquinas nowadays, it is true; but it is not so long ago that textbooks on the Middle Ages could devote appropriate space to Francis, Bernard, and Hildebrand, without so much as a reference to the great Schoolman. Perhaps this is no more than to say that scholars do not make good copy and never have.

If scholars have received something less than their due in Christian criticism and commentary, however, there is a good and familiar reason for it: the deep current of what we today would call anti-intellectualism in Christian tradition. This stream has its source in the New Testament itself. Jesus praises the Father for hiding the religious meaning of life "from the wise and learned and revealing it to the simple-minded." [2] He sees the man of learning as tempted to put stumbling-blocks in the way of piety. "Woe unto you lawyers [or juridical scholars]! You have taken the key that unlocks the door of knowledge; you have not entered yourselves, and you have stopped those who were entering." [3] There are no scholar-heroes in the Gospels. Paul tells the Corinthians that the meaning of the Cross is inevitably unintelligible to the educated Greek mind. God's word is, "I will confound the insight of the wise. Sage, scribe, critic of this world, where are they all? Has not God stultified the wisdom of the world? For when the world with all its wisdom failed to know God in his wisdom, God resolved to save believers by the 'sheer folly' of the Christian mes-

---

COCHRANE, *Christianity and Classical Culture*, London, 1944, pp. 222–223.

[2] Mat. XI: 25. From: *The Bible: A New Translation* by James Moffatt. Copyright 1922, 1935 and 1950—Harper & Brothers. Used by permission.

[3] Luke XI: 52. Moffatt.

sage." [4] "Whoever of you imagines he is wise with this world's wisdom must become a 'fool,' if he is really to be wise." [5] There have always been those, from Tertullian to Christian irrationalists of today, who have gloried in the "sheer folly" and absurdity of the Gospel in the light of the world's reason and resisted all attempts of the learned to demonstrate the reasonableness of Christianity.

There is another current in the New Testament, however, that quietly and indirectly competes with the first. Jesus himself is a profound student of the Scriptures. As Luke records his first public appearance in Nazareth after his baptism and temptation, he announces his mission as the fulfilling of Scripture. [6] There is no talk, as there might have been, of obedience to the voice heard at the Jordan or to visions received in the desert. Jesus is selective in his treatment of Scripture. God is more fully revealed in some parts than in others. And there is a place for interpretation and criticism: "You have heard ... but I say ...." The most obvious thing about the Jesus of the Synoptic Gospels is that he is a teacher who is aware of his relation to a great religious tradition, steeped in that tradition, and conscious of a call to shape it. To this extent, he is a "scholar."

There is a better case, of course, for saying that both John and Paul, not to mention the learned author of the *Epistle to the Hebrews,* are scholars. "In the beginning was the Word ...." The familiar words prefaced a profound attempt to interpret the person and work of Christ in the light of a complex Greek doctrine—or perhaps of an equally sophisticated Essene tradition, if what the recently discovered Dead Sea scrolls suggest is to be accepted. The Fourth Gospel is not only a biography of unparalleled

---

[4] I Cor. I: 19–21. Moffatt.

[5] I Cor. III: 18.

[6] Luke IV: 14–21.

beauty and insight, it is a work of scholarship in the broad-est sense of the word—an attempt to relate the Gospel to its total cultural setting, both Hellenistic and Hebrew. Paul is, of course, a close student of the Hebrew Scriptures. His interpretation of the Old Testament is the basis of all later Christian exegesis. The prophets foresaw Christ; the vicissitudes of Israel and her leaders are "types" of Christ's birth, death and resurrection. From his knowledge of the Hebrew Scriptures and his acquaintance with Hellenistic thought, as illumined by his faith in the risen Christ, Paul fashioned the rudiments of a philosophy of history which related the Incarnation to a long historical preparation and development. In a sense, this was a profound work of scholarship.

This is not to say that St. John and St. Paul can be understood simply by labeling them "scholars." They were, of course, far more than that. They were the first among Christian writers, each in his own way, to begin the task of relating their faith to the religious tradition out of which it sprang as well as to the surrounding secular culture in which it was to fight for a hearing.

It is worthwhile to consider for a moment the general function of scholarship within any religious tradition, and particularly the Christian. At certain times in the develop-ment of a religion, it is necessary for men to stand off from their beliefs and practices, to analyze them and order them, to attempt to understand them better in the light of their origins and growth and conflict with other beliefs and prac-tices. The primary motive here may be the desire to purify the religious tradition itself in a time of corruption. This will call for critical examination of the origins of the tradi-tion and the validity of the faith. Or the motive may be the desire to bring faith into a more fruitful relationship with culture at some moment of crisis in the history of secular civilization. Or finally it may be that the need is felt to re-examine faith in the light of some new discovery of the human mind about the nature of the physical universe or of man himself. The calling of a Christian scholar, then, may be to shoulder any one of the three major tasks just suggested, or some combination of the three: (1) to re-study the Hebraic-Christian tradition itself, (2) to relate this tradition to the surrounding secular culture and its tradition (until modern times, of course, this meant primarily Greco-Roman tradition), and (3) to reconcile faith and science, in the broadest sense of the word. In the period with which we shall be dealing, Christian scholars are most often occupied with the first, least often with the third. The greatest minds, like Augustine and Aquinas, will occupy themselves with all three. But throughout the patristic and medieval periods, the quest for truth is thought of as the *re*covery of what is embedded in tradition, whether religious or secular, rather than the *dis*covery of what is new. This means that the scholar is generally more concerned about relating the New Testament to the Old, or the Bible to classical learning, than he is with reinterpreting the faith in the light of some new view of the cosmos.

This sort of Christian calling is, I grant, neither very dramatic nor very exciting. It is hard to make it appear even significant in comparison with sainthood or prophecy. Paul did not mention scholarship as a church vocation. But when he had done speaking of apostles, prophets, teachers, miracle-workers, healers, and speakers in tongues, he added inter-preters—and it is tempting to think that he may have been saving a place for the scholar.[7] Certainly at various turning-points in the history of Christianity the scholar has had cru-cial influence. One of these was the century or so during

---

[7] I Cor. XII: 29, 30.

which Greco-Roman civilization went into its death-throes. Another was the High Middle Ages. And a third was the age of the Reformation. This chapter is concerned in a very general way with the first two of these periods, later chapters with the third.

In order to gain some sense of the tradition of Christian scholarship, some idea of what it meant to be a Christian and a scholar during the years before the Reformation, let us consider briefly four outstanding examples, two from the late Roman Empire and two from the High Middle Ages. If such a discussion demonstrates nothing else, it will show how hard it is to construct what a sociologist would call a "model" or "type" of the Christian scholar in general. All through this study we shall notice common problems and recurring solutions of various kinds. But the particular balance of attitudes and answers in any given person always contains elements of uniqueness and unpredictability. "Truly, man is an amazingly vain, fickle, and unstable creature, about whom it is hard to establish any constant and uniform judgment," says Montaigne in his first essay. And the historian who tries to establish the very image of a Christian scholar is inclined to agree with him. A varied, changing, but continuous *tradition* of Christian scholarship is, however, a possible object of study, if not of precise definition. Such a tradition can be sensed, if not precisely formulated, by close examination of some of its great bearers.

The student of Christian scholarship during the Reformation is inevitably driven back to Jerome and Augustine, if only because so many later scholars consciously modeled themselves after one or the other (almost never after both, incidentally). With Jerome and Augustine we must begin, therefore. Nearly exact contemporaries, both of them scholars and teachers, each the exact opposite of the other in many ways both serious and amusing, these two Fathers of the Latin Church were destined to become the prototypes of at least two sorts of Christian scholar in later years. We shall consider them with a constant eye upon what later generations were to see in each as a Christian man of learning.

St. Jerome (347?–420 A.D.) was an altogether marvelous combination of contradictory characteristics—of sensuality and asceticism, of irascibility and tenderness, of maliciousness toward his enemies and affection for his friends, of stubborn pride and impulsive humility. But the most significant contradiction within him was his ambivalent attitude toward the pagan classics, the alternate attraction and repulsion he felt for the world of secular learning. The intellectual climate of his day emphasized the inherent contradiction between Christianity and paganism. Christianity as yet had no culture of its own. The children of Christian believers had perforce to learn to read and write in schools which taught grammar, rhetoric, and dialectic through the study of the great pagan classics. The dangers were obvious —the Christian student might fall in love with the classics, as Jerome did—but there was no easy solution. Many Christian leaders, like Tertullian, preached the total incompatibility of Christian belief and pagan culture. A few suggested that Christians might use secular learning as a steppingstone to more intelligent understanding of their faith —if they were careful.[8]

Great scholarship generally stems from a youthful passion for books and for the kind of learning to be found in books. This passion young Jerome had in abundance. We know little about his early life except that he apparently loved the pagan classics and the Christian God of his par-

---

[8] See *A Monument to Saint Jerome,* ed. F. X. MURPHY, New York, 1952, pp. 216 ff., and C. N. COCHRANE, *Christianity and Classical Culture,* 2nd ed., London, 1944, especially Chap. VI.

ents with equal enthusiasm, but not always at the same moment. A modern novelist says of him that "he loved God, learning, and virgins in that order." [9] As a young man who had sown his wild oats with abandon, then started upon a life of ascetic piety with equal enthusiasm, he found it difficult to reconcile his various enthusiasms. The spiritual attraction of the pagan classics became entangled in his mind with the physical temptation of lust, and both were condemned by his conscience. The conflict seems to have come to a head in his famous Vision near Antioch, about 375 A.D. As he wrote of it nine years later, in spite of his resolve to become a Christian ascetic he still had a way, after hours of fasting and vigil, of stealing a look at Cicero or Plautus. (He had taken up the study of the Bible some years before, but in contrast with his beloved pagan writers, the Prophets seemed to him "rude and repellent.") Then came a high fever which wasted him down to skin and bones while he watched the preparations for his own funeral. Suddenly he was caught up in the spirit and dragged before the Judge in blinding light. "Asked who and what I was I replied: 'I am a Christian.' But He who presided said: 'Thou liest, thou art a follower of Cicero and not of Christ. For "where thy treasure is, there will thy heart be also." ' Instantly I became dumb, and amid the strokes of the lash —for He had ordered me to be scourged—I was tortured more severely still by the fire of conscience." Finally Jerome cried out an oath: "Lord, if ever again I possess worldly books, or if ever again I read such, I have denied thee." When he awoke his shoulders were black and blue.[10]

It is tempting to say that this was Jerome's Road to

---

[9] ROBERT PAYNE, *The Fathers of the Western Church*, London, Heineman, 1952, p. 106.
[10] Epistle 22, par. 30 (384 A.D.) in *Saint Jérôme: Lettres*, ed. JÉRÔME LABOURT, 3 vols., Paris, 1949–52. Translation in *St. Jerome: Letters*

Damascus as a Christian scholar. But it was not so simple as that. Jerome was recalling a fevered dream some nine years after the event to clinch the case for asceticism in a long letter to his friend, Eustochium. We know that he loved to exaggerate. Dreams of scourging before the Judgment Seat seem to have been a commonplace with sensitive consciences of the fourth century, a fact which has even led some scholars to wonder whether Jerome made the whole story up. But there seems to be no good reason to doubt that he dreamed his dream.[11] No one else, as far as we know, ever dreamt that his particular sin was "Ciceronianism." In later years he tended to minimize the dream's importance. When his opponent Rufinus twitted him on the fact that he was blithely teaching the classics at Bethlehem twenty-five years after he had promised never to look into a pagan author again, Jerome replied that too much importance should not be attached to dreams. We are not responsible for what takes place in them he said, and we are certainly not obliged to observe an oath made in our sleep, nor to regulate our life by it. It is too simple to call this backsliding or senile decay. The truth seems to be that Jerome, sometime between his Vision and his arrival eleven years later at Bethlehem, had resolved his inner conflict, had found his calling, and could afford to relax and forget some of his earlier compulsions like the oath in his dream. The discovery of his vocation seems to have turned upon the inner conflict dramatized in the dream. And so I think it was a sound instinct that led the artists and scholars of the Middle Ages

---

and Select Works, in *A Select Library of Nicene and Post-Nicene Fathers*, 2nd series, Vol. VI, New York, 1893.
[11] FERDINAND CAVALLERA, *Saint Jérôme*, Paris, 1922, II, 77–78; PAUL MONCEAUX, *Saint Jérôme: sa jeunesse*, Paris, 1932, pp. 119–128; and E. A. QUAIN, "St. Jerome as a Humanist," in *A Monument to St. Jerome*, New York, 1952, pp. 228–229.

and the Renaissance to focus upon Jerome's Vision as a symbol of the man and his work.

Just when or where he found a clear sense of his calling it is impossible to say. Perhaps in the desert immediately after the Vision. Perhaps while studying Origen and the Scriptures with that profound Christian scholar, St. Gregory Nazianzen, in Constantinople. Perhaps not till Pope Damasus summoned him to Rome and commissioned him to revise the Latin translation of the New Testament from the original Greek—the real start of his life's work, as it turned out. Probably it was a gradual process. He says significantly in the account of his Vision, "Thenceforth I read the books of God with a zeal greater than I had given to the books of men." The "thenceforth" is probably deceptive, but the words suggest how Jerome found the solution to his inner problem: *by turning his insatiable appetite for scholarship from one object to another, from the secular to the sacred.*

In 386 A.D. he retired to Bethlehem, set up his curious little community of widow-ladies and disciples, and plunged into his great work of translating the whole Bible and commenting upon much of it. "He is always occupied in reading, always at his books with his whole heart," a friend who visited him reported. "He takes no rest day or night; he is always either reading something or writing something." [12] The torrent of writing that issued from Bethlehem was phenomenal: those brilliant letters that picture contemporary life so vividly and caustically, and discourse about everything from biblical exegesis to the

---

[12] SULPITIUS SEVERUS (quoting POSTUMIANUS), Dialogue I, chap. 9, in *A Select Library of Nicene ... Fathers*, Second Series, Vol. XI, New York, 1894. On Jerome's principles of translation, see W. SCHWARZ, *Principles and Problems of Biblical Translation*, Cambridge University, 1955, pp. 26–37.

beauties of virginity and how to bring up daughters; theological polemics and large historical works; but above all, the great translations of the various books of the Old Testament from the original Hebrew (his version of the New Testament was merely a revision) with their lively prefaces arguing the importance of getting back to the original sources.

It seems clear from the letters and prefaces of his early years at Bethlehem that he had a sense of having found his calling. In 394 he writes to a young friend Paulinus: "A mind willing to learn deserves commendation even when it has no teacher. What is of importance to me is not what you find but what you seek to find." Paul studied the Law and the Prophets at the feet of Gamaliel "and was glad he had done so." John was no mere untaught fisherman—if so, how could he have written about the Logos, God's Wisdom? He closes his letter by apologizing for being "carried away by his love of the Scriptures" in writing all this, but urges Paulinus to live among these sacred books, meditate on them, know and seek nothing else but them.[13] In his Preface to *Samuel* and *Kings* he writes that everyone offers for the service of God's tabernacle what he can—some, gold, silver, or precious stones; others, linen of various hues. As for him, he will be content to offer "skins and goat's hair" to cover the tabernacle and protect it from sun and rain—his translation, in other words.[14]

Some twenty years after his Vision, he had found a solution of the conflict between his Christianity and his love of secular literature. To Magnus, who reproached him for quoting so often from pagan authors, he gave a long list of Hebrew and Christian writers who had done the same, including Moses and Paul. Paul, he said, knew the command

---

[13] Ep. 53.
[14] *Letters and Select Works*, VI, 489–490.

in Deuteronomy (21:10 ff.) that "when a captive woman had had her head shaved, her eye-brows and all her hair cut off, and her nails pared, she might then be taken to wife." So Jerome had taken secular learning to wife, he says, after "shaving off and cutting away all in her that is dead, whether this be idolatry, pleasure, error, or lust," in the confidence that his "so-called defilement with an alien" would increase the population of Christians.[15]

As a scholar, Jerome was enormously learned, insatiably interested in words and names, marvelously well equipped linguistically—he pointed out proudly that he was "trilingual," in Latin, Greek, and Hebrew. All his life he was driven by an inexhaustible desire to learn, to know, and to write. An unkind modern critic avers that "even to gain Paradise, he would have hesitated to sacrifice one *bon mot*."[16] He was slipshod and slapdash in his methods, touchy under criticism, and too quick to turn his genius for picturesque invective against an opponent. Like all great scholars, he had profound respect for the difficulty and complexity of his subject and poured some of his most picturesque contempt on the "gossipy old women, old men in their dotage, and long-winded sophists" who thought they could interpret Scripture with no linguistic equipment and no intellectual training. "Others—oh, the shame of it!—learn from women what they teach to men."[17] The interpretation and translation of Scripture was his passion. His work, the Vulgate, is one of the supreme achievements of Christian scholarship. To this Latin translation he applied the best tools of contemporary secular scholarship. Through it he

---

[15] Ep. 70 (397 A.D.). About fourteen years earlier he had interpreted the same passage in the same way in writing Pope Damasus. See Ep. 21, par. 13.

[16] MONCEAUX, *op. cit.*, p. 237.

[17] Ep. 53, par. 7.

opened up many of the nuances of Hebrew and Greek religious insight to the Latin Christian mind and so became one of the founders of a Christian culture in the West.

He was no theologian or philosopher. His mind was empirical rather than speculative, haunted by history rather than by abstract ideas. He loved the minutiae of philology, but he was impatient with the minutiae of creeds and confessions. When his fellow monks in the desert tried to draw him into a controversy on the Trinity by questioning his orthodoxy, Jerome wrote somewhat naively: "Every day I am asked for a confession of faith, as if I had never made any when I was baptized. I confess whatever they like: they are not satisfied. I sign my name: they still don't believe me." [18]

He died in 420, near-blind and despondent, his little monastic community recently sacked by the Pelagians, his spirits weighed down by the Sack of Rome ten years before. But his spirit was to be reborn more than once in the history of Christian scholarship. His particular way of reconciling his lust for learning with his devotion to God and His Word was to exercise great influence on a certain type of Christian mind in centuries to come. His zest for biblical translation and elucidation, his insistence on getting back to the literary sources, his concern for philological detail as the basis of correct understanding ("it is one thing to be a prophet and another to be a translator," he wrote), his respect for the difficulties involved, and the belief he lived out in his own life that scholarship is a Christian calling of high dignity and significance—all these things were to have their rebirth in the age of the Reformation.

Perhaps we need say less of St. Augustine (354–430 A.D.) because his towering figure is more familiar than that

---

[18] Cotidie exposcor fidem, quasi sine fide renatus sim. Confiteor ut volunt: non placet. Subscribo: non credunt. Ep. 17, par. 3.

of Jerome.[19] His importance for our purposes is this: in his life and writings he dramatized for future generations of Christian scholars the truth that in all the important areas of knowledge a man cannot know unless he believes. *Nisi crederitis, non intelligetis*—unless you believe, you will not come to know—became the foundation-stone of intellectual enterprise in Christian Europe for a thousand years after Augustine. "If you cannot understand, believe in order that you may understand." [20] Mind working by reason cannot attain to truth unless assisted by the *lumen Dei*, the divine illumining. This, of course, was no advocacy of blind faith. It was the testimony of one of the greatest minds in Christian history to the fact that truth can never be grasped by a man's mind alone. It must be seized by the whole of him, must satisfy his every part. And this can never happen unless there is a leap of faith at the start. It is the *lumen Dei* that makes intellectual vision possible.

Augustine began with as avid a thirst for learning as Jerome. The *Confessions* suggest that he was just as deeply stirred by the pagan classics as Jerome had been, although perhaps in a different way. His first reading of Cicero's *Hortensius* in his nineteenth year made an extraordinary impression on him. It was not Cicero's style but his matter that moved him. "This book, in truth, changed my affections and turned my prayers to Thyself, O Lord, and made me have other hopes and desires." It inflamed him with "the love of wisdom," he tells us, at a time when he was too

---

[19] For what follows, see particularly VERNON J. BOURKE, *Augustine's Quest for Wisdom*, Milwaukee, Bruce Publishing Co., 1944; and WHITNEY J. OATES, ed., *The Basic Writings of Saint Augustine*, 2 vols., New York, Random House, 1948. The quotations which follow are from this edition by permission of the publishers.

[20] *Sermo* 118, quoted in *A Monument to St. Augustine*, London, 1930, p. 159.

self-centered to appreciate the Scriptures.[21] A year later he devoured Aristotle and was able to understand what he read "without any great difficulty," he says, "and without the teaching of any man." But it did him no good because it penetrated no deeper than his mind. "Both quickness of comprehension and acuteness of perception" are God's gifts, he recognized, but unless God adds the gift of His illumination, they may serve as readily to a man's destruction as to his use.[22] In the end, Augustine like Jerome came to terms with the pagan writers and wrote a classic defense of Christian Humanism in his book *On Christian Instruction*. But the two men thought of secular learning in characteristically different ways. To Jerome pagan learning was a captive woman who drew him by her charms and whom he would marry if the law allowed. To Augustine it was gold and silver, like the spoil which the children of Israel were commanded to take with them out of Egypt and turn to better use. Here were "liberal arts readily adapted to truth, and very useful principles of morality." [23] In these two stark figures of lust and theft legitimized, the Middle Ages found most of the arguments they needed for a Christian Humanism.

Augustine, however, saw a profounder relationship between secular studies and Christian insight. As he looked back upon it, it was God who had led him along his intellectual odyssey from the confusion of his early years through Manichaeanism to Neo-Platonism and finally to Christianity. In a passage of amazingly subtle self-analysis, Augustine developed the idea that the very chronological order in which he had come upon the Neo-Platonic writings and then

---

[21] *Confessions*, Book III, chap. 4.

[22] *Confessions* IV, 16.

[23] *De Doctrina Christiana*, Book II, chap. 40. Cf. QUAIN in *A Monument to St. Jerome*, pp. 220–223.

the Holy Scriptures was significant and providential. It was God's will, he thought, that he should begin with Platonism and remember its effects upon him after his conversion to Christianity. Thus he would be sensible of the difference "between those who saw whither they were to go, yet saw not the way [i.e., the Platonists], and the way [of Scripture] which leadeth not only to behold but to inhabit the blessed country." If he had taken the Scriptures to heart first, he thought, he might either have been seduced by later coming upon the Platonic writings, or have been convinced that he would eventually have arrived at Christianity simply by studying Platonism alone.[24] In other words, if the order of his intellectual and spiritual development had been otherwise, he might either have stumbled or fallen into intellectual pride.

There are some points worth noting about the famous conversion experience itself. It took place at Milan in 386 A.D., about eleven years after Jerome's Vision at Antioch. Augustine was already an intellectual convert to Christianity, but his will had not been brought round until the agony in the garden under the fig tree. "What is wrong with us?" he said to Alypius. "The unlearned start up and 'take' heaven, and we with our learning but wanting heart, see where we wallow in flesh and blood." [25] In the moment of decision, the learned and unlearned are no more than equal, with some advantage to the unlearned. Learning as such is irrelevant to salvation. And yet the youthful voice said "Take up and read"; and it was a verse from St. Paul upon which the saint's last resistance was broken. The mind played its part, even in the crisis. When it was all over, the one symbolic act which he felt it necessary to take (besides renouncing marriage) was quietly to resign his Professor-

---

[24] *Confessions* VII, 20.
[25] *Confessions* VIII, 8.

ship of Rhetoric as a sign of his "election" to serve God. But he did not thereby renounce learning.

In fact, Augustine's conversion was the beginning of one of the most prolific writing careers in Christian history. His immediate retirement to Cassiciacum and the conversations there with friends upon the nature of wisdom and the possibility of knowing truth were in the best classical tradition of fostering the life of the mind through leisurely discourse. Through the conversations ran Augustine's deepening conviction that he had found the key to knowledge, his belief that a believer *can* know. He could not have written, as Jerome did, that what a man finds is not so important as what he seeks to find. A wise man cannot be satisfied with the search for wisdom; he must some day find it. "Just how human wisdom is constituted, I do not see as yet. But since I am only in my thirty-third year, I don't think that I should despair of its eventual attainment. I intend to continue my search .... It is now my conviction that what I want most is *to grasp the truth, not by belief alone but also by understanding.*" [26]

In other words, while Augustine's conversion impressed upon him (and upon his later readers) the essential irrelevance of learning to salvation, it launched him upon a lifelong career of study and writing. The result was one of the most comprehensive and enduring attempts to understand the Christian faith which has ever been made. Augustine developed a specifically Christian ethic as an alternative to the veiled Stoicism of the Pelagians. He elaborated the first Christian philosophy of history in answer to those who held that Christians were ultimately responsible for the Sack of Rome by Alaric in 410. He worked out a theory of the Church and a theology of grace which remained in equilibrium with each other through the Middle Ages until they

[26] *Contra Academicos* III, 20, 43, in VERNON J. BOURKE, *op. cit.*, p. 74.

split apart during the Reformation (the Catholics holding to his theory of the Church and the Protestants building upon his theology of grace). He built Neo-Platonism into the structure of Christian thought and became the true founder of Christian philosophy. The thirst for knowledge of his youth was thus transmuted into a vast program of study and interpretation based upon the implicit belief that religious conversion and moral integrity are the indispensable conditions of scholarly achievement. To Augustine there could be no such thing as a purely secular search for truth: "If wisdom is God, who made all things, then the philosopher is a lover of God." [27] He found his calling as a scholar sometime soon after his conversion. To put it into our words, not his, this calling was to capitalize upon the wide range of his intellectual Odyssey and the depth of his religious experience to become the mediator between classicism and Christianity at the moment of ancient civilization's disintegration.

The contrast with Jerome was evident enough. At the risk of grossly oversimplifying, we may try to sum up the differences. Jerome, in spite of his visions, seems to have been a "once-born" Christian; Augustine was "twice-born." Jerome was a philologist, a lover of words and language; Augustine, a philosopher, a lover of ideas. Jerome was fascinated and sometimes overwhelmed by mundane reality; Augustine concentrated upon God and the soul. Jerome saw the danger in pagan learning; Augustine saw the danger in learning itself. Jerome was impressed by the complexity of reality and the need of often suspending judgment; Augustine moved through scepticism to assurance and even to dogmatism. For over twenty years (394–416) the two argued over scriptural interpretation by correspondence across half the Mediterranean. Augustine believed that

---

[27] *City of God*, Book VIII, chap. I.

the *Septuagint* was an inspired translation of the Old Testament into Greek, of equal authority with the Hebrew, if not greater. Jerome based himself upon philological analysis of the Hebrew. Augustine was particularly troubled by Jerome's insinuation that St. Paul was, on one occasion at least, a liar. Jerome was not one to take such criticism lying down, of course, and the controversy was boiling merrily when Jerome finally decided that it was making a bad impression on heretics and called it off. "I have decided to love you," he wrote Augustine.[28] Jerome was a great scholar who was a Christian; Augustine was a great Christian who left an indelible mark on scholarship. The two are the main archetypes of the Christian scholar, if archetypes there are.

If we leap ahead seven centuries, our attention will be attracted to two of the most interesting scholars of the High Middle Ages, Peter Abelard (1079–1142) and St. Thomas Aquinas (1225–1274). In them we shall find two archetypes of a different sort, not necessarily parallel to the two we have just considered.

From the point of view of intellectual history, the first half of the twelfth century was the most exciting fifty years since the fall of Rome.[29] The long fight for sheer survival had finally been won and Europe was beginning to feel her energies overflow. The Crusades had begun, and Western European scholars were traveling in Spain, Sicily, and Asia

---

[28] JEROME, *Letters and Select Works*, VI, *passim*. Cf. VERNON J. BOURKE, *op. cit.*, pp. 150–152; W. SCHWARZ, *op. cit.*, pp. 37–44.

[29] On what follows, see C. H. HASKINS, *The Renaissance of the Twelfth Century*, Cambridge, 1928, pp. 47–48, 351–381; HELEN WADDELL, *The Wandering Scholars*, 4th ed., Boston and New York, 1929, pp. 104–111; A. C. McGIFFERT, *A History of Christian Thought*, New York, Scribners, 1933, II, 201–221; and particularly RICHARD P. McKEON, "Renaissance and Method in Philosophy," *Studies in the History of Ideas*, New York, Columbia University Press, III (1935), 37–114.

Minor, ransacking Moslem libraries, and translating into Latin the scientific and philosophical works of the ancient Greeks, preserved and commented upon by the Arabs. The intellectual excitement was widespread, but Paris soon became its focus. In the twelfth century Paris became "a city of teachers," the first the medieval word had known.[30] And the teacher who attracted most students, stirred up most intellectual ferment, exasperated most fellow-teachers, and had the most enduring influence, was Peter Abelard.

Abelard is an important example in the history of Christian scholarship of a man whose work was greater than himself. There is a certain autonomy of the mind and the spirit, a certain independence of intellectual achievement and moral excellence, which we ignore at our peril if we are to understand the history of Christian scholarship. It may be that Abelard was never stirred by anything but worldly motives all his life—though I think this is an unfair judgment. His concerns were Christian concerns, however, and he left an indelible mark on Christian scholarship. To use the dogmatic analogy, the scholarly graces mediated through him were valid in spite of the state of his own soul. In him the scholarly office was greater than the man.

In his *History of his own Calamities*[31] he gives, without realizing it, a devastating portrait of himself. He wrote it, he says, to cheer up an afflicted friend by showing him how much worse his, Abelard's, troubles were than his friend's. It is the portrait of one who tried to bring his passion for

---

[30] H. RASHDALL, *The Universities of Europe in the Middle Ages*, Oxford, 1895, I, 289.

[31] Latin text edited by J. T. MUCKLE, "Abelard's Letter of Consolation to a Friend," *Mediaeval Studies*, XII (1950), 175–211. Trans. J. T. MUCKLE, *The Story of Abelard's Adversities*, Toronto, 1954, with useful notes. I have sometimes followed the phrasing of the livelier translation of C. K. SCOTT MONCRIEFF in *The Letters of Abelard and Heloise*, New York, Knopf, 1926.

learning under the control of his Christian ideals and failed
—and knew that he had failed. Apparently he came to believe in a kind of one-to-one correspondence between scholarly achievement on the one hand and moral purity and
humility on the other, a correspondence which he was utterly
unable to realize in his own life and which was somehow
belied by the results of his work. He gave up a feudal
noble's inheritance to satisfy his voracious appetite for learning. As a student he was not popular with his teachers in
Paris. He was too bright for them, badgered them in class
and made snide remarks about them out of class. Finally he
set up shop on his own as a teacher and stole pupils in droves
from his former mentors. Apparently he turned from logic
to theology for reasons of ambition. Theology was queen
of the sciences, and he knew he could make more of a reputation as a theologian than as a logician. He sneered so loudly
at his first theological teacher's knowledge of Scripture that
he was maneuvered into announcing that he himself would
lecture on Ezekiel, although he had never studied the book.
The lecture was a huge success, but the teacher was not impressed and said so. "So by persecution," Abelard remarked,
"my fame increased."

He made a poorer case for his tragic love-affair with
Heloise than later generations might make. It began in
what we would call a common enthusiasm for learning and
flowered into romantic love of real nobility. But in looking
back on it, he could see only pride, lust, and retribution. He
pictured pride and lust as the cause of his downfall not only
as a Christian but also as a scholar. Puffed with intellectual
arrogance, he was an easy victim for the temptation of lust,
he tells us. The further he advanced in intellectual grasp of
philosophy or the Scriptures, the further he receded from
the great philosophers and divines, who had "excelled especially by the grace of continence." His love for Heloise

made him neglect his work until he became a mere reciter of things he had learned in the past. When Heloise became a mother and Abelard offered to marry her, Heloise argued that there was a clear connection between celibacy and achievement in philosophy down through the ages; Socrates was wedded, it is true, she said, but that was "a defilement of philosophy"; Abelard was "created for all mankind," she insisted, and it would be "disgraceful," "lamentable," if he dedicated himself to one single woman. They were married, however, in secret. But her uncle's fear that Abelard meant to desert her led to the brutal attack upon him by her relatives. Thus his lust, he writes, was ended by his castration; his pride was soon to be broken by the condemnation and burning by a Church council of his most-prized book. (Just how his intellectual pride was broken by a judgment which he considered utterly unjust—as it was—he never quite explains.) At any rate, he accepted the consoling advice of his friends that his misfortune was providential in that it had "set him free from carnal snares" so that he could devote himself without distraction to sacred duties. He became a monk and at the end of his account he is in a remote Breton monastery, convinced that his fellow monks are trying to poison him and his enemies lying in wait for him outside the walls.

Incidentally, in this calamitous history, Abelard often refers to Jerome. As Jerome was driven by the Romans to the East, so Abelard says he was driven by the French to the West, from Paris to Brittany. His trials seem to him like those of Jerome, "whose inheritor I esteem myself in the slander of detraction." The idea that there is a one-to-one relationship between celibacy and intellectual achievement, which he both expresses himself and puts into the mouth of Heloise, he drew from Jerome.[32]

At first glance, ambition and accident appear to account

---

[32] See MUCKLE in *Mediaeval Studies*, XII (1950), 173–174. Abelard

for Abelard's career as a Christian scholar. But the matter cannot rest there. This erratic, sick soul was one of the most extraordinary teachers of whom we have record and his writings influenced everyone who read or thought at all in the High Middle Ages. What he wrote seems to have grown directly out of his teaching. To make his students think before they jumped to conclusions, to encourage them to understand what they believed, he wrote a discussion of the Trinity (the book that was condemned), a large treatise on Christian theology and a briefer introduction for students, a book on ethics (in which he was particularly interested), a dialogue between a philosopher, a Jew, and a Christian (designed to argue the superiority of Christianity to natural law and to Judaism), and above all, his *Sic et Non.* In the preface to this last he said that his purpose was to stimulate young readers to search out the truth for themselves. "For by doubting we come to inquiry, by inquiry we discover the truth," he wrote, in oft-quoted words. In the body of the work he lined up 1,800 conflicting opinions of the Church Fathers pro and con on 158 propositions of theology and ethics, such as "That faith is to be supported by human reason, and the contrary—That to God all things are possible, and not—That it is lawful to kill a man, and not." No conclusions were drawn. The student was invited to come to his own. It was not that Abelard thought his questions could not be answered. Many of them he answered himself by dialectical method in his other works on theology. But to assemble all the conflicting texts on any given problem and to understand them—this was the first step. Elsewhere he summed up the central belief of his life by quoting Ecclesiasticus to the effect that "he that believes quickly is light-minded." [33]

seems to have dressed up Heloise's arguments with his own references to Jerome and others.

[33] McGiffert, *op. cit.,* II, 216; McKeon, *loc. cit.,* 65–69.

What Abelard did through his teaching and writing was to make his generation think—and think hard—about the Christian faith at a very important moment in Western history. This was the moment when a young European society was awakening to self-consciousness and to the awareness that there were alternatives to Christianity, in Islam, and back of Islam, in ancient Greece. Abelard argued that the Christian faith must be able to defend itself, must be reasoned, if not also reasonable. I can offer no evidence that he had any very high religious view of his calling as a scholar. Perhaps one critic is right who says he was simply "a scholar for scholarship's sake." [34] But I think one could argue that he thought of himself as a sort of Socratic gadfly commissioned by God to stir the noble steed of Christendom to life. At least it is easy to imagine him revising Socrates and saying that "the unexamined faith is not worth believing." He was not a thorough-going rationalist. Revelation was still his bed-rock. Scripture was to be taken as authority, as also the Fathers—when they agreed. It is by simple faith that men are saved, not by reason. The Christian proceeds from faith to understanding, he does not come to faith through understanding. But when he succeeds in attaining to understanding, Abelard adds, it is a delightful experience. The liberal arts—grammar, rhetoric, and especially dialectic—are of great importance for the understanding of Scripture and the Fathers. In fact, the saints who had a thorough education in the liberal arts before their conversion, he points out, had greater command of sacred learning after their conversion. Paul, for instance, had greater grace in doctrine after his call than Peter.[35]

Abelard was one of the chief authors of that sustained and systematic application of reason to the data of revelation

---

[34] WADDELL, *op. cit.*, p. 106.
[35] McKEON, *loc. cit.*, 61, referring to *Theologia Christiana*, Book III, in Migne, *PL*, 178, 1213.

that we call Scholasticism. His method of compiling, comparing, and evaluating texts was followed by Peter Lombard, who wrote the most influential theological textbook of the Middle Ages. He forged the weapons which Aquinas tempered and used so effectively some hundred years after his death. In spite of his personal failings, he belongs in the front rank of Christian scholars.

A century after Abelard's death the teachers of Paris had organized themselves into a "university," but their lives were almost as turbulent, their quarrels almost as violent, as they had been in Abelard's day. Above all, the critical question raised by Abelard had not yet been answered: would Christianity be able to absorb the new intellectual influences, particularly Aristotle, or would it succumb in the end to these influences? It was Thomas Aquinas who, more than anyone else, transformed Aristotelianism from Christian threat to Christian asset. From the rather meager data we have about his life and personality, it seems clear that never were a man and his work more closely identified, nor never a man better fitted for his job. To reconcile Aristotle and the Bible was a large order. More precisely, to steer between the dangerous enthusiasm for Aristotle of the faculty of arts at Paris and the narrow contempt for him of the faculty of theology (which was Augustinian and Platonist) demanded the brilliance of a great mind and the patience of a saint, the insight of a first-rate scholar and the devotion of a practising Christian. And this is what the task fortunately called forth: "The saintliest of the learned and the most learned of the saints." [36]

Thomas was a tall, dark, hulking man who had inexhaust-

---

[36] On what follows, see ANTON C. PEGIS, ed., *The Basic Writings of Saint Thomas Aquinas*, New York, Random House, 1945; JACQUES MARITAIN, *St. Thomas Aquinas*, London, Sheed, 1931; MCGIFFERT, *op. cit.*, pp. 257–294; and JOHN F. MCCORMICK, *St. Thomas and the Life of Learning*, Milwaukee, 1937.

ible mental energy, enormous powers of concentration, incredible emotional balance, and a striking single-mindedness about his calling. At the trial of his canonization fifty years after his death, he was described as "soft-spoken, easy in conversation, cheerful and bland in countenance; good in soul, generous in conduct; most patient, most prudent...." [37] In his mid-teens he decided to become a Dominican, against the shocked opposition of his noble family. He took the habit in 1244, but was kidnapped by his brothers at their mother's orders and detained for a year at home. One of his brothers tried in vain, we are told, to tempt him with "a young and pretty damsel," but he remained chaste to his death and his dying confession was said to be like that of a child of five.

Thomas eventually left his native Naples to study at Paris and Cologne with the greatest scholar of his day, Albertus Magnus. In 1256 at the age of thirty-one he was called by the University of Paris to be made Doctor of Divinity and to teach theology. Thomas held back. There was hatred of the Dominicans in the University, he knew, and he had the scholar's fear of publicity and dislike of controversy. He prostrated himself before the altar and, thinking of the parlous state of affairs in the University, began to recite the Latin of the twelfth Psalm: "Save me, O Lord, for thy truths are vanishing from the children of men." "He prayed and wept for a long time, then fell asleep. And behold he saw a heavenly messenger appear before him in the form of a certain old and venerable Brother of his own Order, who said to him: 'Friar Thomas, why these prayers and tears?' He replied: 'Because they are going to make me a Master and my knowledge is not equal to it. And what subject to take for my inaugural address I know not.' The old man replied: 'Behold your prayer is heard. Take up the re-

[37] MARITAIN, *op. cit.*, p. 37.

sponsibility of the doctorate. God is with you. For your inaugural expound only these words [from Psalm 104]:
"Thou waterest the hills from thy high chambers; the earth
shall be filled with the fruit of thy works." ' " [38] Thomas
arose refreshed and lightened and took up the burden of
teaching, disputation, and writing which he was not to lay
down until a few months before his early death eighteen
years later in his forty-ninth year.

His production during these years was almost unbeliev-
able. No inner conflict, no self-pity, no subjective strife held
him back from his chosen life's work of demonstrating that
reason and revelation point toward the same truth, and that
man through his senses and his reason may reach a long
way up to the hand that reaches down to him in grace.
Legends, perhaps with a kernel of truth to them, grew up
about his energy and devotion. He worked incessantly, we
hear, could dictate to four secretaries on four different subjects, drop off for a nap, and continue to dictate in his sleep.
"It was not so much to the effort of his mind that he was
beholden for his learning," said his disciple Reginald, "as
to the force of his prayers." Before study or writing, before
debate or teaching, he would pray in secret; and if he ran
head-on into an insoluble point, he would carry his doubts
before the altar, stand sobbing a while, then return to his
cell to record the solution. He constructed probably the
greatest theological system ever devised by a Christian mind
and yet three months before his death a change came over
him and he remarked to Reginald, "I can do no more; such
things have been revealed to me that everything I have
written seems to me rubbish." [39]

There is no question in the case of Aquinas of the unity of

---

[38] WILLIAM of TOCCO's account, quoted in R. B. VAUGHAN, *The Life
and Labors of S. Thomas of Aquin*, Albany, 1874, p. 496, note.
[39] MARITAIN, *op. cit.*, pp. 44–46, 51.

the man and the work. Whether describing the man himself or his writings, later commentators are driven to employ the same descriptive terms: sanity, balance, moderation, thoroughness, comprehensiveness, breadth of mind. To Aquinas, God is never arbitrary—and as a scholar he himself was never arbitrary. There was a grand objectivity about all his work that seemed to stem from the resolution of all internal conflict. He wrote no history of his own calamities. Having once carried his own sense of inadequacy to his calling before the altar, he thenceforth carried there only the problems of his age, or of his scholarship, or of his Church and University, so far as we know. He searched out the critical theological questions of his day, marshalled all the arguments on both sides of each from his wide learning, then unlike Abelard, relying on his prayers and his God-given reason, he would intervene at the proper moment with his resounding *Respondeo dicendum* ... and the question was settled. He accepted Abelard's challenge. By inquiry he *reached* the truth.

These, then, are some of the ways in which God calls a man to be a scholar, the tasks He puts the scholar to, and the way the scholar responds to His call. Jerome, Augustine, Abelard, and Aquinas—each was called in a different way to assume one or more of the three major tasks of a Christian scholar: to restudy the Hebraic-Christian tradition itself, to relate this tradition to secular culture, to relate this tradition to scientific discovery. They exemplify the variety rather than the uniformity of scholarship as a Christian calling. The only excuse for selection of these four rather than dozens of others is that they appear to be the most fundamental prototypes, to be imitated consciously or half-consciously by later generations of Christian scholars. Each lived on in his books—Jerome particularly in his *Letters*, Augustine in his *Confessions*, Abelard in his *Sic et Non*,

Aquinas in his *Summa Theologica*—and in each a question was embodied of the sort that must be answered anew by each succeeding generation of Christians: What has Athens to do with Jerusalem, Cicero with Christ? Can a man know unless he begins with belief? Can critical intelligence be safely applied to Christian faith? Is it possible to synthesize Christianity and culture? These questions were still very much alive in what enthusiasts have called "The Revival of Learning."

The Revival of Learning:

From Petrarch to Colet

MODERN critical scholarship, like modern experimental science, may be said to have originated in intellectual movements of the later Middle Ages. The remote origins of both intellectual disciplines, of course, lie in ancient Greece, but the continuous development of each in its modern Western form began with Petrarch and William of Ockham respectively. Just as something like the modern scientist's interests and attitude toward nature began to appear in the sceptical, inquiring, empirical attitudes of Ockham's followers at Paris and (later) Padua, so something like the modern scholar's mental presuppositions and critical weapons began to emerge in Petrarch's successors in Florence and Rome during the fifteenth century and north of the Alps during the sixteenth century. Scholarship as we know it is the product of what an older generation of historians called "The Revival of Learning."

We need not pause here to argue the aptness of the term. Obviously, it does something less than justice to the science and philosophy of the High Middle Ages to talk about *the* Revival of Learning in Italy after Petrarch. The phrase is used here in a purely descriptive sense, to characterize the considerable increase in the numbers as well as the zeal of scholars interested in Greek and Roman literature and philosophy which was such a striking feature of Italian history in the fourteenth and fifteenth centuries. Considered thus, the Revival of Learning was a social change which can be measured in quantitative terms. But it was also an intellectual revolution of considerable complexity and importance.

It is difficult in the twentieth century to understand the unbridled enthusiasm with which educated persons in Italy searched out, read, and discussed the Greek and Roman literary classics in the two centuries between the death of Dante (1321) and the death of Machiavelli (1527). It is easier to understand if we remember that a social as well as an intellectual revolution was in progress. Nowhere in Europe were the middle classes so self-conscious and so powerful in local politics as in the wealthy cities of Northern Italy, yet until the classical revival they had no culture they could really call their own. To the merchants and bankers, the lawyers and civil servants of cities like Venice, Florence, and Milan, the chivalric culture of the feudal nobility was always something alien, unrelated to their deepest interests. The same was true of the scholastic learning of the clergy. But Cicero and Virgil, Plato and Aristotle, had written for an urban society not unlike their own. The ancient historians, philosophers, and poets were concerned about civic, moral, and aesthetic problems, about man and society, and how to live well in this world. All this struck a respondent chord in the mercantile and professional people of Northern Italy, and eventually of all Europe. Like science three centuries later, the classics seemed to satisfy some deep inarticulate need. Here was a lay culture of extraordinary variety and fascination, long hidden beneath the imposing structure of a clerical scholasticism. No wonder that clerics and laymen alike ransacked monasteries to turn up classical manuscripts, copied assiduously, and commented interminably on what they found. By the fifteenth century there was an eager audience for their findings. A man could now make his living as a classical scholar—teaching the children of rich merchants, writing dispatches for a city government or turning out poetry for some wealthy patron—and this was something new.

There were other indications of social change. In the Dark Ages the monasteries had been the centers of learning in Europe. In the High Middle Ages it was the Cathedral and its schools, which sometimes became a university. Now it was the princely court or the wealthy urban patron. By the early sixteenth century the great printing establishment would be added to the court as a meeting-place for men of learning. Libraries began to grow at a rate unheard of since classical times, at first by the activity of copyists, then through the acquisition of printed books. Manuscript books in the fifteenth century were the object of reverence, sought and bought at high prices, bargained for in peace settlements, stolen by predatory scholars. The books chosen for libraries showed the influence of three revivals: a revival of classical Latin which began in the fourteenth century, a Greek revival which began in the early fifteenth, and a Hebrew revival which began in the late fifteenth. By 1500 a good Latinist could find as many jobs open to him as a psychologist today; a mediocre Graecist could find students eager to pay him almost anywhere in Europe; and any sort of Hebraist at all could cause a stir by hanging out his scholarly shingle. In the hottest part of a Paris summer a young Italian Humanist, Aleander, announced a series of lectures on a third-rate Roman poet, Ausonius. Two thousand people turned out for the first lecture and listened for two hours and a half—according to the lecturer, with no signs of fatigue. On the third day, all the seats were taken at eleven o'clock although the lecture did not begin until one. It is a famous story not because it was unusual, but because it was fairly typical of the Humanist and his audience during the classical revival.[1]

These more external and evident marks of the Revival of Learning were accompanied by more subtle changes in attitude which amounted to an intellectual revolution. In its simplest terms, this revolution consisted in a shift within the spectrum of the three primary liberal arts that were the nurture of all scholars, a shift from dialectic as the key discipline toward grammar and rhetoric. To Abelard, as to Aquinas, dialectic was the queen of the liberal arts, grammar and rhetoric her hand-maidens. Truth to them was a structure of true propositions about God, man, and nature. In order to arrive at one of these propositions, Abelard's first step was to pose a problem and then to assemble all the statements he could find in the Bible, the Fathers, or the ancient philosophers which bore upon it. The second step was relatively simple and unimportant: to determine by the use of grammar just what each statement meant. The final step was all-important, especially in Aquinas: to examine conflicts, to winnow the true from the false, and to sift out the truth in propositional form through the careful use of dialectic as developed by ancient philosophers, particularly Aristotle, and as recommended by Christian

---

[1] P. S. ALLEN, *The Age of Erasmus*, Oxford, 1914, pp. 112–113. On the subject of the scholarly revival in general, see MYRON P. GILMORE, *The World of Humanism*, New York, 1952, Chap. VII.

Fathers such as Augustine. It goes without saying that the medieval Schoolman was more a philosopher than a historian.

The classical revival brought with it a fundamental change in scholars' minds as to the nature and objectives of scholarship itself. While Abelard culled passages to support or destroy propositions, Petrarch read (and became enthusiastic about) whole works of ancient writers. Abelard subordinated grammar and rhetoric to dialectic; Petrarch and his followers subordinated dialectic to grammar or rhetoric. The study of words and of style, the analysis of how a language is put together and what it may be made to do, the examination of an author in relation to his audience and the whole purpose of his work—these became increasingly the preoccupations of scholars. It is significant that the commonest meaning of "scholar" in Elizabethan English was one versed in Greek and Latin literature. The Revival of Learning thus meant a shift of interest from philosophy to philology, from logic to literature, from abstract truth to concrete, personal fact. In Richard McKeon's words, it was the "subversion of dialectic to grammar." The author and the reader became more important than the timeless, impersonal argument. "The new emphasis was upon the document and the writer, rather than upon the doctrine and the tradition .... What was sought was light rather than doctrine, love rather than knowledge, letter rather than principle." [2]

Perhaps the most important result of this shift in scholarly interest and emphasis was the development of a new sense of historical perspective, the birth (or rebirth) of the sense

---

[2] RICHARD McKEON, "Renaissance and Method in Philosophy," *Studies in the History of Ideas*, New York, Columbia University Press, 1935, III, 62, 67–71, 75, 79–89, 93–95. The body of this essay is a penetrating comparison of Abelard, Erasmus, and Luther.

of anachronism. The medieval Schoolmen's preoccupation with timeless and abstract truth reflected the underdeveloped historical sense of the Middle Ages. There was little sense of significant change in time so long as men believed that only the eternal and unchanging was ultimately important. Gothic art reveals the fact that to ·the medieval artist pagan antiquity was still in some sense alive. Julius Caesar and Alexander were dressed in medieval armor because no one felt that there had been any essential breach in historical continuity. Frederick Barbarossa was still "Roman Emperor," there was still a "Romanorum Imperium." The mere passage of time between Caesar and Barbarossa, of which writers were aware, was not significant. The classical past was still contemporary. But something began to happen to this view in the century after Dante's death. Petrarch was apparently the first to talk of a "Dark Age" that lay between his own day and classical antiquity. Imperceptibly a whole new sense of the past, a new sense of temporal perspective, was born at about the same time that Italian painters began to represent figures in spatial perspective. There had been a *Romanorum Imperium*, scholars like Leonardo Bruni and Flavio Biondo began to see, but it had "declined" and been succeeded by a "Dark Age," after which there had been a "revival" or "rebirth" of civic culture. Thus the sense of anachronism was revived. The Caesars had now to be represented in togas, in temporal as well as spatial perspective. The continuity was gone, but classical antiquity could now be grasped and comprehended as a cultural whole by three new-born intellectual disciplines: history, archaeology, and philology. "The classical world ceased to be both a possession and a menace," as it had been to Gothic minds, writes Panofsky; instead, it became "the object of an everlasting nostalgia .... The pre-Gothic Middle Ages had left Antiquity unburied and alternately galvanized and exorcised its body. The Renaissance stood weeping at its grave and tried to resurrect its soul." [3]

The implications of all this for the scholar who took his commitment to the Christian religion seriously were confused and unclear at first. It had not been easy to domesticate Greek philosophy in medieval Christianity, but Aquinas and others had done it. Abelard had found Christian uses for dialectic but was suspicious of grammar and rhetoric: "What has Horace to do with the Psalter, Virgil with the Gospel, Cicero with the Apostle?" he asked, echoing Jerome. [4] The line of least resistance for the Christian Humanist was to castigate dialectic (and Scholasticism in general) as unchristian, to ask with Erasmus what has Aristotle to do with Christ, and to sing the praises of grammar and rhetoric as potential allies of Christian belief. This the Humanists did, from Petrarch on, but it was not so easy to persuade either themselves or others as it might have seemed. And it is this that gives the study of the Christian scholar and his calling during the Reformation its interest. For one thing, to reject Abelard and Aquinas was to be driven back to the equally fundamental questions raised by Jerome and Augustine as scholars and Christians. And to think more and more as historians and less and less as philosophers was to raise a disturbingly new question for Christian thinkers: What if there had been a breach of historical continuity within Christianity

---

[3] ERWIN PANOFSKY, "Renaissance and Renascences," *Kenyon Review*, VI, no. 2 (Spring 1944), 227–228, and *passim*. See also T. E. MOMMSEN, "Petrarch's Conception of the Dark Ages," *Speculum*, XVIII (1942), 226–242; and MYRON P. GILMORE, "Fides et Eruditio: Erasmus and the Study of History," in *Teachers of History: Essays in Honor of Laurence Bradford Packard*, Ithaca, 1954, pp. 17–24. On philology as a "layman's science," see W. K. FERGUSON, "Renaissance Tendencies in the Religious Thought of Erasmus," *Journal of the History of Ideas*, XV (1954), 505.

[4] MCKEON, *loc. cit.*, pp. 62, 79. Abelard referred to Jerome, Ep. 22.

itself, a breach between a primitive apostolic Church close to its Founder's spirit and a corrupted institution of a later and darker age which had unwittingly broken the tie that bound it to Christ? What if the new history, archaeology, and philology should appear to shake to its foundations the structure of Christianity as a set of timeless beliefs? There was work enough for Christian scholars to do as a result of the Revival of Learning.

To suggest some of the facets of the problem we must select and concentrate as we did in the preceding chapter. The most important figures to understand if one would know something of the impact of the Revival of Learning upon the Christian scholar and his sense of calling are Petrarch, Lorenzo Valla, Pico della Mirandola, and John Colet. With these four we shall be concerned in this chapter.

Francesco Petrarca, or Petrarch (1304–1374), was the first to feel deeply the personal implications of the new scholarly interests and perspectives which we have discussed —or at least the first to be articulate about his doubts and worries. More clearly than anyone of his generation, Petrarch was able to conceive Roman antiquity historically, as it had been, a pagan society of infinite attractiveness. He knew this society was dead, but he found by experience that he could revive its greatest figures and their thoughts in his imagination and live in spiritual friendship with them. This gave peculiar poignancy to his sense of the gulf between the *Respublica Romana* and the *Respublica Christiana*, between civic and monastic ideals, between Cicero and Christ. He knew that the Voice might reproach him for being a Ciceronian rather than a Christian as it had reproached Jerome. But characteristically, it was an imaginative literary dialogue, not a vision, in which the conflict within him took place between his love for pagan antiquity and his devotion to Christianity. This was his *Secret*, the famous dialogue between St. Augustine and himself which he wrote in 1342 at the age of thirty-eight and always kept by his bedside to remind him of his soul-searchings at the height of his intellectual powers. The problem is Jerome's primarily, but the Father who Petrarch feels will best understand his own passions and problems is not Jerome but the author of the *Confessions*. The Augustine of the dialogue is a curious mixture, part Augustine as he was, part Petrarch's prudish medieval conscience. He is always right in his argument with Petrarch's more human half, but he is not always understanding enough of human failings. He wins the argument but loses Petrarch's soul.

Petrarch's *Secret* is an extraordinarily subtle piece of self-analysis. Augustine lays bare Petrarch's spiritual anatomy with the relentless touch of a skilled soul-surgeon: his infatuation for Laura, which Augustine insists was never so high-minded or ennobling an affair as Petrarch maintains it was; his ambition for literary fame, which the saint says is more soaring and limitless than Petrarch is aware of; and his *accidia,* his inner melancholy and malaise, the result of a hopelessly divided mind and will. When Petrarch blames all these failings on external circumstances and agencies, Augustine brings him relentlessly back to their internal roots. The trouble is "your overcrowded mind," he says; you have "no considered plan"; you "can never put your whole strength to anything" because of the "worrying torment of a mind angry with itself [which] loathes its own defilements, yet cleanses them not away." Read Seneca or Cicero, he says, or for that matter read your own book on *Tranquillity of Soul;* you are "a past-master in the whole field," but like too many other writers of your generation, you do not practice what you preach.[5]

The root of the trouble, it develops, is a deep dichotomy

---

[5] *Petrarch's Secret* .... trans. WM. H. DRAPER, London, Chatto and Windus, 1911, pp. 45–46, 99, 138. The quotations that follow are used by permission.

between occupation and conscience. No man of his generation was ever more engrossed and seduced by the pleasures
of scholarship and writing than Petrarch. All his life he
sought some satisfying moral justification of the work he
loved—in vain. He quoted Cicero's definition of glory to
Augustine—"the illustrious and world-wide renown of good
services rendered to one's fellow-citizens, to one's country,
or to all mankind"—with the implication that this was what
he was doing. But Augustine was not taken in: "Why and
wherefore, I ask, this perpetual toil, these ceaseless vigils,
and this intense application to study? You will answer, perhaps, that you seek to find out what is profitable for life. But
you have long since learned what is needful for life and for
death. What was now required of you was to try and put
in practice what you know, instead of plunging deeper and
deeper into laborious inquiries, where new problems are always meeting you, and insoluble mysteries, in which you
never reach the end .... You write books on others, but
yourself you quite forget." [6] Does this mean, asks Petrarch,
that I must drop my work entirely? Yes, says Augustine,
Rome has been celebrated before; think only on your ap-
proaching death. Petrarch says he wishes Augustine had
told him all this earlier. "I will pull myself together and
collect my scattered wits, and make a great endeavor to
possess my soul in patience," he concludes, "but I have
not strength to resist that old bent for study altogether."
The "true order" is "that mortal men should first care for
mortal things, and that to things transitory, things eternal
should succeed." Meanwhile he prays that God will lead
him "safe and whole out of so many crooked ways." [7]

In the course of the dialogue, Petrarch raised anew the
question which had haunted both Augustine and Abelard,

[6] *Ibid.*, pp. 166–170.
[7] *Ibid.*, pp. 176, 184–192.

the question of the relation between learning and goodness, or more precisely, the problem of scholarship and sex: can a sinner be a good scholar? "Remember," says Augustine to Petrarch on the subject of Laura, "remember how ill your profession accords with a life like this; think how this woman has injured your soul, your body, your fortune." [8]

The whole question of learning and goodness came up again twenty-five years later in an amusing way. In 1366 four Venetian noblemen amused themselves after a good dinner by debating and declaring a formal legal sentence to the effect that Petrarch was certainly a good man but a poor scholar, "a good man without learning." This cut Petrarch to the quick. He waited a year, then wrote an elaborate answer in the classical form of an invective entitled *On my own ignorance and that of many others*. His line of defence—ignoring for the moment the various layers of irony—is that he may not know much but neither does anybody, and he is at least a devoted Christian, which is more than his enemies can say. At the same time he is careful to display his erudition by saturating the essay with classical quotations. Furthermore, he sketches the reply *he* would make if he were to be accused of Ciceronianism as Jerome was: "My incorruptible treasure and the superior part of my soul is with Christ; but because of the frailties and burdens of mortal life, which are not only difficult to bear but difficult merely to enumerate, I cannot, I confess, lift up, however ardently I should wish, the inferior parts of my soul, in which the irascible and concupiscible appetites are located." Cicero has done him no harm and much good, he insists. Augustine and Jerome both had the same experience. "I even feel sure that Cicero himself would have been a Christian if he had been able to see Christ and to comprehend his doctrine," he adds, as Augustine had

---

[8] *Ibid.*, p. 163.

thought of Plato.[9] Yet in all this there is no real justification of the scholarly or literary calling. In fact there is a deep undercurrent of anti-intellectualism which seems more than merely ironical: "It is safer to strive for a good and pious will than for a capable and clear intellect. ... It is better to will the good than to know the truth. ... In this life it is impossible to know God in his fulness; piously and ardently to love Him is possible. ..." [10] "It will be enough if I succeed in being wise within the limits of sobriety; and this can be achieved without much learning, even without any, as is clearly shown by the long line of illiterate saints of both sexes." [11] And yet Petrarch spent years of his life working over a scholarly book *On Illustrious Men* of classical antiquity and had really very little love for "illiterate saints."

It is too easy to make fun of Petrarch. A badly integrated personality, we would say today—and send him to the psychoanalyst's couch. But Petrarch's emotional tensions were the warning of a new era in the history of Christian scholarship. The particular kind of reconciliation between classicism and Christianity which was represented by Aquinas in philosophy, Dante in poetry, and the Gothic Cathedral in art could not last forever because it was based on hazy and inaccurate notions of the past, both classical and Christian. The rise of history, archaeology, and philology as scholarly disciplines was bound to sharpen the differences between Athens and Jerusalem and reveal the shaky historical foundations of the so-called medieval synthesis of Greek

---

[9] *The Renaissance Philosophy of Man,* ed. ERNST CASSIRER, P. O. KRISTELLER, and J. H. RANDALL, Chicago, University of Chicago Press, 1948, pp. 113–115. Copyright 1948 by the University of Chicago. The quotations that follow from Petrarch and Pico are used by permission.
[10] *Ibid.,* p. 105.
[11] *Ibid.,* p. 127.

reason and Christian faith. As the philological and historical attitudes spread, they would reveal that the gulf between the classical point of view and the Christian was far wider than either Aquinas or Dante suspected. What Petrarch did was to dramatize and popularize these new scholarly attitudes. Elaboration of the disciplines themselves he left to others, but he did demonstrate vividly the psychological tensions that might result if the disciplines were taken seriously. Try as he might, Petrarch could never quite bring his scholarly activity and his Christian faith into any organic relationship with each other. He could never gain a sense of calling as a Christian and a scholar. His failure was an omen of how difficult the task was to be in the next two centuries of growing secularism and deepening religious strife.

The destructive possibilities, both for good and ill, of the new attitudes which accompanied the Revival of Learning became abundantly evident a century after Petrarch in the career of Lorenzo Valla (1405–1457).[12] Valla exemplified better than anyone else of his generation the triumph of grammar and rhetoric over dialectic, of the historical over the philosophical attitude. He had probably the keenest critical intelligence of any of the Italian Humanists. Like Jerome he was primarily a philologist—and like Jerome he was always getting into violent literary quarrels. Like Abelard he seems to have been primarily concerned to make his generation think, question, ponder its unexamined beliefs and assumptions.

His book *On the Elegancies of the Latin Language* (published 1444) was for its day a model of the best critical

---

[12] There is no recent critical study of Valla. See the overenthusiastic but useful account of GIROLAMO MANCINI, *Vita di Lorenzo Valla*, Florence, 1891. A. RENAUDET offers a brief but penetrating sketch in *La fin du moyen-âge*, Paris, 1931, I, 513 ff.

method in linguistic study and served as the foundation of good Latin style and sound method for later Humanists, notably Erasmus. Unlike Jerome, Valla's restless intellect applied the methods learned in philology to the criticism of doctrines and institutions. At twenty-six years of age he wrote a dialogue *On Pleasure* which attacked Petrarch's naive reconciliation of Stoicism with Christian ethics, questioned the validity of good works as a conscious moral goal and suggested ironically that a life lived according to Epicurean principles was a better introduction than Stoicism to the eternal bliss reserved for Christians. Soon he was applying his criticism to Scholasticism and monasticism. The Schoolmen, he said, really did not know their Aristotle, and they wrote very bad and obscure Latin; they should have paid more attention to rhetoric than to dialectic, which was after all a barren method. The monks, he said, had falsely usurped the name of "religious" and were trying to dodge the secular duties demanded of all Christians; there was only one moral perfection, he insisted, open to layman and cleric alike; the monks were rather a sect than a religion. His most famous work was his conclusive proof, on historical and philological grounds, that the *Donation of Constantine,* upon which so much of the papal claim to temporal power was based, was an arrant forgery. Typical of his method were his remarks about the "satraps" which the author of the document incautiously mentioned. "What have satraps got to do with the case?" asks the outraged historian and philologist. "Numskull, blockhead! Do Caesars speak thus? Are Roman decrees usually drafted thus? Whoever heard of satraps being mentioned in the councils of the Romans?" [13]

If the new criticism could be applied to the *Donation of Constantine,* why could it not be applied equally well to

---

[13] *The Treatise of Lorenzo Valla on the Donation of Constantine,* trans. C. B. COLEMAN, New Haven, Yale University Press, pp. 84–85.

other documents of the Christian tradition? Valla's originality lay in his insight that if collation of manuscripts,
analysis of language, and examination of historical context got one closer to the mind of Cicero or of Aristotle,
the same techniques would presumably get one closer to the
mind of the Fathers, or of St. Paul, or perhaps of Moses. No
document was so sacred as to be exempt from philological
analysis, providing that fundamental doctrines were not
questioned. Valla demonstrated that a letter from King Ab-
gar of Edessa to Jesus was apocryphal. He proved that the
mystical writings attributed to Dionysius the Areopagite
could not possibly have been written by a contemporary of
St. Paul's, as generations of medieval students had believed.
He argued that the Apostles' Creed was the work not of
the Apostles but of the Council of Nicaea. But most important of all, he took in hand three Latin and three Greek
codices of the New Testament and demonstrated that the
Latin Vulgate was full of grammatical misunderstandings
and unhappy translations. Paul had written extremely well
in Greek, he pointed out; it was a shame that his meaning
was so often twisted or obscured by the translator. He
could not believe that the New Testament Vulgate was
Jerome's work. Jerome was too good a scholar and stylist
for that. The New Testament verses scattered through his
works are always better translated than they are in the Vulgate. Either Jerome had nothing to do with it, or the copyists had ruined his work.

We have no evidence that Valla ever published these
"Notes on the New Testament," [14] which he finished about
1444 and revised some eight years later. To all intents and

---

[14] *In novum testamentum ex diversorum utriusque linguae codicum col-
latione adnotationes,* first published by Erasmus at Paris in 1505. I have
used the 1541 edition cited below. See MANCINI, *op. cit.,* pp. 238–243;
W. SCHWARZ, *Principles and Problems of Biblical Translation,* Cambridge University, 1955, pp. 132–134.

purposes, the "Notes" were what might be called "pure scholarship." The author was concerned exclusively with words not with doctrine, with expression rather than content. His procedure was to take a phrase from the Latin, compare it with the Greek, point out the error or obscurity and suggest a better translation. On Romans 1: 17, for instance, the verse that became the starting-point of Luther's new understanding of Paul, Valla says laconically: " 'The just live by faith': 'live' should read 'shall live.' " [15] Even where an emendation might suggest theological implications, Valla sticks closely to linguistics, as in his comment on Romans 7: 24, 25: " 'O wretched man that I am, who shall deliver me from the body of this death? The grace of God through Jesus Christ our Lord': It is not 'of God' but 'to God,' that is, 'thanks be to God' .... I think it should be interpreted 'Thanks be to God, who himself delivers us through Jesus Christ.' " [16] On Romans 10: 5, in a typical reconstruction, he unscrambles what Moses said from what Paul said in the same confused Latin sentence.[17] To the reader of the "Notes," there is a shrewd but thoroughly non-theological mind at work. Valla had a pointed message for theologians, however—namely, that theologians are not exempt from the disciplines of grammar and rhetoric. "Some people deny that Theology is subject to the rules of grammar, but I say that theologians ought to obey the rules of a language, whether written or spoken. In fact what is more stupid than to wish to corrupt the language you use and make yourself unintelligible to those whom you are addressing!" [18]

---

[15] *Lavrentii Vallae .... in Nouum Testamentum Annotationes .... cum Erasmi Praefatione ....* , Basel, 1541, fol. 133.

[16] *Ibid.*, fol. 137v.

[17] *Ibid.*, fol. 140.

[18] *Ibid.*, fol. 12.

The "Notes" inevitably raise the question of Valla's motives. Was all this a subtle attack on Christian belief, or was it an attempt to cleanse and purify the Christian faith? Was Valla a sceptic or a believer? There is no simple and easy answer to the question. It used to be the fashion to say that Valla's writings made sense only on the assumption that his was an emancipated and "modern" mind, sceptical not only of superstitious practices but also of the truth of Christianity itself. More recently those who know Valla's writings best have come to agree that his loyalties were definitely Christian. In this view, the attacks on the temporal power of the Papacy, on Scholasticism and monasticism, on the Latin Vulgate, were all in the interest of a simplified, purified, and more ethical Christianity. He was indifferent to the neo-paganism and scientific scepticism of his day. Just as a man of the twentieth century may accept democracy as his birthright and yet criticize its abuses sharply, so Valla accepted Christianity and yet wished to chastise it by what one writer calls a "philological crusade" against dialectic, a crusade on behalf of Scripture and the Fathers against the Averroists and Ockhamists of his day. Another commentator sees moral passion in all his attempts to set the record straight, and religious zeal in his attack on the *Donation of Constantine*.[19]

The doubt remains, however. Valla's life-long ambition, eventually fulfilled, was to become a papal secretary. It is not impossible that his writings were partly motivated by the desire to show off his learning and eloquence. Ethical

---

[19] RENAUDET, *loc. cit.*, represents the view that Valla was fundamentally secular in his viewpoint. In contrast, see MANCINI, *op. cit.*, pp. 327–328; GIUSEPPE TOFFANIN, *History of Humanism*, New York, 1954, pp. 159–167; C. E. TRINKAUS, JR., in *The Renaissance Philosophy of Man*, ed. CASSIRER, KRISTELLER, and RANDALL, Chicago, 1948, pp. 147–154; and H. J. GRIMM, "Lorenzo Valla's Christianity," *Church History*, XVIII (June 1949), 75–88.

earnestness and religious piety were not prominent parts of his make-up, though courage and intellectual honesty were. There is no trace of evidence that he felt any tension between his scholarly tastes and his Christian belief, as Jerome and Petrarch did. In the preface to Book IV of his *Elegancies of the Latin Language* he launched a vigorous attack on those who argued from Jerome's Vision that Christians should never read secular writers, with never a hint that he really understood Jerome's psychological conflict. Apparently any conflicts that he experienced were external ones. He seemed to relish a good fight. Once, to clear himself from the suspicion of heresy, he preached a sermon to the Congregation of the Dominicans in Rome. The sermon was supposed to be in praise of St. Thomas, the greatest of Dominican scholars, but the speaker made it quite clear that he preferred Paul and the early Fathers to Thomas and his dialectics. "This is a slippery and dangerous place for me," he said. "What may I do about it? Reform, reverse, conceal what I believe? But the tongue would disagree with the heart." [20] He had the instincts of a true critic, writes his biographer: "to compare, to judge, to illuminate, to correct, to show literature the way to become a supremely effective force in ameliorating society." [21] But how much of this could be called Christian motivation we shall never know and it is useless to inquire. To assess the precise extent to which an individual mind or a whole society has become what we call "secularized" is the most difficult problem the historian of this period has to face. Valla never protested his Christian motives in the way Abelard and Petrarch felt called upon to do; nor did he ever proclaim his contempt for Christianity. His work exemplifies nicely how faint and fluctuating is the line that

---

[20] *The Renaissance Philosophy of Man*, pp. 151–152.
[21] MANCINI, *op. cit.*, p. 331.

separates the religious from the secular in the motivation of critical scholarship at the close of the Middle Ages. What Valla did as a scholar was indispensable to Erasmus, Luther, and Calvin—and they all spoke well of him. He demonstrated what historical and philological criticism could accomplish. But we will never be able to fathom the combination of worldly motives, disinterested love of truth, and Christian aims, that inspired his work.

The ideal scholar, if there were one, would be composed of equal parts of critical ability and appreciative capacity. The two are not often united in the same man. Valla was long on critical acumen but short on appreciative insight (into Scholasticism, for instance). The most spectacular scholar of the next generation, Giovanni Pico della Mirandola (1463–1494),[22] was long on the power of appreciation and short on critical penetration. Valla was a philologist who had little patience with philosophy; Pico, a philosopher who had no great interest in philology. If Valla illustrated the benefits and potential dangers of criticism, Pico demonstrated the strengths and weaknesses of a sort of indiscriminate appreciation as the foundation of scholarly work.

It is hard to describe Pico and make him believable. The attempt somehow reminds one of that remark of Montaigne's about stories of the same witch appearing one day in one place and the next a thousand miles away: "To tell the truth I would not believe my own eyes in such a case." [23] Apparently Pico had everything: brains, good looks, noble birth, money, ambition, and enormous energy. Above all, he had an insatiable thirst for learning, which he attempted

---

[22] The best treatment of Pico is E. GARIN, *Giovanni Pico della Mirandola: Vita e Dottrina,* Florence, 1937. See also *Giovanni Pico della Mirandola: His Life by his Nephew Giovanni Francesco Pico,* trans. SIR THOMAS MORE, ed. J. M. RIGGS, London, 1890.
[23] *Essays,* III, 11.

to slake at Bologna, Padua, Florence, Rome, and Paris. In 1486 at the tender age of twenty-four—"full of pride and desirous of glory," his nephew-biographer tells us—he went to Rome and published nine hundred Theses or propositions drawn from the lore of all ages and places, Eastern and Western. To the startled scholarly world he proposed to defend these propositions before all comers and offered to pay the traveling expenses of any debaters who should come from a distance. The Pope was unimpressed. "This young man wants someone to burn him some day," he remarked. A papal commission censured thirteen of the propositions—such as that Christ did not really and truly descend into Hell but only *quoad effectum,* and that no one's beliefs are simply the product of his will alone. Pico wrote a hasty *Apology* but this got him into more trouble. He fled to Paris where he was imprisoned for a short time, then escaped to Florence where he remained under the protection of Lorenzo de' Medici during most of his few remaining years. This conflict with ecclesiastical authority shook him deeply. Looking back on it, he told his nephew he thought it was by God's special providence that he had thus been falsely accused of heresy so that he would come to his senses, give up "the voluptuous use of women," to which he had been addicted, and correct his evil ways. Just what the character of this "conversion" was, it is hard to say. He sold his hereditary lands, burned some youthful love poetry, and talked of going out barefoot to preach Christ—after he finished writing "certain books" he had in hand. He came increasingly under the influence of Savonarola, who insisted in a sermon preached after his death that Pico had determined to become a Dominican friar. But he remained a layman, and except that he concentrated somewhat more on purely religious problems, the change in his life apparently did not affect his whole conception of learning, as it had

Augustine's. In 1494 at the early age of thirty-one he died of a fever in three days of illness.

Pico's technical accomplishments as a scholar were prodigious. He knew Latin, Greek, Hebrew, and Arabic. Unlike Petrarch and Valla, he had great respect for Scholasticism on the ground that in spite of all barbarism of style and technique, it was a method of getting at truth. He had an extraordinary memory and could read through whole stacks of books with incredible speed, according to his nephew. In the delightful translation of Sir Thomas More (on whom Pico's life made a deep impression), this nephew sums up the "five causes that in so short time brought him to so marvelous cunning: . . . first, an incredible wit, secondly a marvelous fast memory, thirdly great substance [which helped him to buy books], [fourth] his busy and infatigable study, [and fifth] the contempt [and] despising of all earthly things." [24]

This enormous ability and energy never quite found a focus before Pico's untimely death. In the nine hundred Theses and in the famous *Oration* which prefaced them he showed an undiscriminating, almost Gargantuan intellectual appetite for anything knowable. In his *Heptaplus* (1489) the subject was the first twenty-six verses of Genesis, but the discussion ranged over the whole spectrum of contemporary learning. In *De Ente et Uno* (1491) the immediate object was to reconcile Plato and Aristotle, but the real subject was the nature of truth. In the last years of his life he told his nephew that only the Bible satisfied him and that he would concentrate upon biblical study alone except that he felt an obligation to the public to get out the many major works he had worked on for so long. He contemplated a commentary on the New Testament and an elaborate apology for Christianity which he never finished.

---

[24] *Pico: His Life*, trans. THOS. MORE, p. 16.

Unlike the case of Valla, there is no question of Pico's personal devotion to Christ in his later years; but there is considerable question about his significance as a scholar and thinker. In effect, he tried to do for his generation what Aquinas did for his (he was a particular admirer of St. Thomas). But the task was harder, there were more intellectual ingredients which had to go into a synthesis, the temper of the age was less favorable to such efforts, and Pico was really not up to the job as a thinker. Ignoring the critical tools of history and philology already developed by men like Valla, he turned back to the allegorical and mystical interpretation of texts developed centuries earlier by Alexandrian scholars. Only thus could he refine out the nuggets of universal truth contained in such disparate writings as the Koran, the Cabala, Plato, Aristotle, and the Bible and show to his own satisfaction that Zoroaster, Moses, Pythagoras and Christ all said essentially the same thing, if only one knew how to read the texts. He took the first two words of Genesis, for instance—*In principio*—played with various combinations of the letters composing their Hebrew equivalent, and came up with a mystic sentence pregnant with the whole meaning of creation and human history: "Pater in Filio et per Filium, principium et finem, sive quietem, creavit caput, ignem, et fundamentum magni hominis foedere bono." [25] This was what Moses *really* meant to say when he said "In the beginning . . . ." It is clear what one commentator means when he says that Pico was totally lacking in a sense of humor. The same commentator concludes that Pico's thought is "the wildest possible jumble of incompatible ideas, which not even the most dexterous legerdemain can twist into the remotest semblance of congruity." [26]

---

[25] *Ibid.*, p. xviii.
[26] Riggs, *ibid.*, pp. xiv, xxxvii.

This "legerdemain" has recently been accomplished, how-ever,—and accomplished quite convincingly—by a great Renaissance scholar, Ernst Cassirer.[27] He sees an "obscure linkage" of ideas (the phrase is Pico's: *occulta concatenatio*) running through all of Pico's thought. This is the connection of the idea of freedom and the idea of diversity. In the well-known opening paragraphs of his *Oration* Pico pic-tures the peculiar dignity of man, as distinct from every other being, as residing in the limitless freedom to make of himself what he will, to rise to the divine or sink to the bestial. In the pages that follow he gives a humorless de-fense of his daring in publishing the nine hundred Theses although only twenty-four years old and goes on to develop a most interesting argument for freedom of thought. "Just as bodily energy is strengthened by gymnastic exercise, so beyond doubt in this wrestling-place of letters, as it were, energy of mind becomes far stronger and more vigorous." He protests that he has no axe to grind. He is not out to make money (he forgets to add that he does not have to), and belongs to no philosophical school. "Pledged to the doctrines of no man, I have ranged through all the masters of philosophy, investigated all books, and come to know all schools . . . . Surely it is the part of a narrow mind to have confined itself within a single Porch or Academy. Nor can one rightly choose what suits oneself from all of them who has not first come to be familiar with them all. Consider, in addition, that there is in each school something distinctive that is not common to the others." There follows a re-markable paragraph in which he suggests the characteristic and unique virtues of some twenty-odd Greek, Arabic, and Christian thinkers. "What were the gain," he concludes, "if only the philosophy of the Latins were investigated . . . if

[27] In "Giovanni Pico della Mirandola," *Journal of the History of Ideas*, III (1942), 123–144 and 319–346. Particularly pp. 131, 327–328, 337.

the Greek and Arabian philosophers were left out—since all wisdom has flowed from the East to the Greeks and from the Greeks to us?" [28] Pico had something of the same sense of the infinite variety of creatures, ideas, and things in the universe that Montaigne revealed in secularized form a century later. In another sense, he was the Toynbee of the fifteenth century, consciously shaking his contemporaries out of their cultural provincialism. To Pico, an idea, like a person, had an individual dignity and validity, whether it came from Ancient Egypt or from contemporary Italy. Compulsion in matters of belief is morally wrong and practically futile. Truth emerges in discussion, debate, and conflict. Pico took freedom of the mind more seriously than any thinker before him for centuries, and rejoiced in the infinite richness and variety which he found in the world of ideas. "Liberty above all things he loved," wrote his nephew, "to which both his own natural affection and the study of philosophy inclined him." [29]

This wide-angled scholarship without focus was an important product of the Revival of Learning. Like Giordano Bruno's universe, its center was everywhere, its periphery nowhere.[30] We have suggested its strength and need not enlarge on its weaknesses. Pico once paid a Sicilian Jew an outrageous sum for some cabalistic manuscripts. When he had devoured them, he "saw in them (as God is my witness) not so much the Mosaic as the Christian religion"—Trinity, Incarnation, Atonement, Purgatory, and Hell—"the *same things* we read daily in Paul and Dionysius, in Jerome and Augustine." [31] Pico had a great and capa-

---

[28] "Oration on the Dignity of Man," in *The Renaissance Philosophy of Man*, University of Chicago Press, 1948, pp. 240–244.
[29] *Pico: His Life*, trans. THOS. MORE, p. 22.
[30] Cf. CASSIRER, *loc. cit.*, p. 337.
[31] "Oration," *loc. cit.*, p. 252. Italics added.

cious mind, but he had need of discrimination as well as of humor. In his syncretism he almost forgot the unique, the peculiar, the distinct.

One thing is evident. Pico was no more able than Petrarch or Valla to attain any clear sense of calling as a Christian scholar. Petrarch never found any final reconciliation between the Ciceronian and Christian halves of his split personality. Valla never made explicit the Christian roots (if there were any) of his philological crusade. Pico's personal devotion to Christ, the only-begotten Son, never found any adequate place in his vast and indiscriminate syncretism. All three considered themselves scholars and Christians, but none of the three had any consciousness, so far as I have been able to discover, of organic relationship between personal piety and scholarly endeavor.

Here, it would seem, is the importance of John Colet (1467?–1519).[32] Colet was the first to be able to absorb a good deal of the philological and historical interests and attitudes of the New Learning and to direct them to a purpose fully Christian. In him personal piety and professional purpose interpenetrated each other so thoroughly that when his friends wrote about him, the scholar always recalled the Christian and the Christian the scholar. "In London there is John Colet, Dean of St. Paul's, who has combined great learning with a marvellous piety," Erasmus wrote to a friend. Later he said that he had never seen "a more highly-gifted intellect," adding immediately that Colet liked to

---

[32] The primary authority is Erasmus' sketch, in P. S. ALLEN, *Opus Epistolarum Erasmi*, Oxford, 1906–47, IV, Ep. 1211, pp. 507–527; trans. by J. H. LUPTON in *The Lives of Jehan Vitrier ... and John Colet ... by Erasmus*, London, 1883 [hereafter: ERASMUS, *Vitrier and Colet*]. Also J. H. LUPTON, *A Life of John Colet*, London, 1887; and FREDERIC SEEBOHM, *The Oxford Reformers*, London, Everyman, 1914 (1st ed. 1867). The *Life of Colet* by J. A. R. MARRIOTT, London, 1933, adds nothing.

bend this intellect to what would fit him for immortality. At table, Erasmus reported, his conversation was "all either about literature or about Christ." "A book was ever his companion on the road, and his talk was always of Christ." Thomas More said of him after his death: "None more learned or more holy has lived among us for many ages past." [33]

The thing that strikes the historian most about Colet at this distance is the extraordinary balance and harmony in him between conflicting impulses and aims which tore other men of his generation to pieces—or made hypocrites of them. In a little devotional tract that he wrote, an admonition to the reader is repeated like a refrain: order your life "by reason and grace." And its last words are: "Use well temporal things. Desire eternal things. Finis." [34] The balance between this world and the next in his mind gave him an inner assurance that made those who knew him best rely on him for judgment and courage. He had the power, as Lupton notes, "of uniting and attaching others to himself, or rather of drawing them through himself to a higher object." [35] He did not come by this emotional stability easily. "It was but a very small portion of this religious spirit that he owed to nature," Erasmus thought. By nature he was irascible, covetous, and inclined to sensuous pleasures. He had to discipline these three weaknesses all his life, "by philosophy and sacred studies, watching, fasting, and prayer"—that is, by both mind and will. His anger sometimes blazed out in righteous indignation. He founded

---

[33] Erasmus to Servatius Roger, 8 July 1514, ALLEN, *Opus Epistolarum,* I, Ep. 296; ERASMUS, *Vitrier and Colet,* pp. 31–32, 26; Thomas More to a Monk, 1519–20, *The Correspondence of Sir Thomas More,* ed. ELIZABETH F. ROGERS, Princeton, 1947, p. 192.

[34] "A ryght fruitfull monicion concernynge the order of a good christen mannes lyfe," in LUPTON, *Life,* pp. 305–310.

[35] LUPTON, *Life,* p. 265.

St. Paul's School with the money he inherited from his wealthy merchant father, partly because he knew his tendency to covetousness. He never married (he was ordained priest in 1498) and his dinners were notoriously frugal, "yet," says Erasmus, "if an occasion ever presented itself, either of conversing with ladies, or being a guest at sumptuous repasts, you might have seen some traces of the old nature in him." Erasmus concluded the warm pen-portrait which is the chief source of our knowledge of Colet's life by remarking that although he never noted any sign of human weakness in his saintly friend Vitrier, "In Colet were some traits which showed him to be but man." [36]

Colet was not a saint. He was a tall, graceful, vigorous, enthusiastic person, gifted with a nice combination of ease of manner and seriousness of purpose, who somewhere along the way decided not to follow in the footsteps of his father, a prosperous mercer who was twice Lord Mayor of London, but to devote himself to sacred studies. It would be good to know more about this decision—when it was made, whether all at once or slowly, how hard a thing it was, and what it meant. We know only that he went up to Oxford in his 'teens with a zest for learning, took his M.A. there, and then "like a merchant seeking goodly wares," in Erasmus' words, "he visited France, then Italy," probably between 1492 and 1496. For a generation Englishmen with studious tastes had been going to the homeland of the Revival of Learning to study Latin and Greek, as well as medicine and law. Two of them, Thomas Linacre and William Grocyn, had returned and were teaching at Oxford while Colet was there. We know almost nothing definite about Colet's sojourn in Italy. Erasmus says that "while there he devoted himself entirely to the study of the sacred writers," which suggests that his purpose was already settled before he went

---

[36] ERASMUS, *Vitrier and Colet*, pp. 30–31, 46.

abroad. He already knew the early Fathers and the chief Schoolmen and had been perfecting his command of English by studying the English poets, "preparing himself, even at this date, for preaching the Gospel," says Erasmus. We may infer that like Erasmus after him, he was impressed by the moral corruption he saw in Italy but not by the architecture and painting. He may have met Savonarola and Pico's fellow-scholar, Marsiglio Ficino, perhaps even Pico himself before his death in 1494. But we do not know.[37]

The only thing of which we are reasonably sure is that he came back with the feeling that he had something to say to the educated circles of his own country. After a brief visit with his parents in London he returned to Oxford. There in the fall of 1496 he announced a series of public lectures on the Epistles of St. Paul. He was barely thirty years old, not yet a Doctor of Divinity, but the whole learned community turned out to hear him, doctors and students alike.

These lectures on I Corinthians and Romans were a milestone in the history of Christian scholarship.[38] Probably no one can really appreciate their freshness and originality who has not turned over page after page of medieval commentaries on Scripture, as patient modern scholars have done.[39]

---

[37] ERASMUS, *Vitrier and Colet*, p. 22; LUPTON, *Life*, pp. 45–58. On the date of Colet's visit to Italy, see W. K. FERGUSON in *Amer. Historical Review*, XXXIX (1934), 696–699.

[38] See particularly P. ALBERT DUHAMEL, "The Oxford Lectures of John Colet," *Journal of the History of Ideas*, XIV (Oct. 1953), 493–510. Duhamel places Colet in the framework of McKeon's thesis (see above, note 2). Also LUPTON, *Life*, pp. 59–87; and SEEBOHM, *op. cit.*, pp. 17–24. Lupton has edited Colet's lectures and other writings in John Colet, *An Exposition of St. Paul's Epistle to the Romans*, London, 1873; *An Exposition of St. Paul's First Epistle to the Corinthians*, London, 1874; *Letters to Radulphus ... with other treatises* [including the second "Exposition of St. Paul's Epistle to the Romans"], London, 1876.

[39] On what follows see BERYL SMALLEY, *The Study of the Bible in the*

To be sure, there was penetration and considerable variety of approach in medieval commentary. Thanks to the influence of Jewish scholars on Christian commentators, the literal or historical sense was never lost sight of and grammatical analysis survived. Aquinas maintained that the literal sense must always be the basis of all exegesis. But early medieval scholars were fascinated by the allegorical and anagogical (or mystical) meanings of Scripture. And more important, as Scholasticism developed, the Bible came to be looked upon more and more as merely grist for the dialectician's mill, as we have seen. The Old and New Testaments were fragmentized, treated as "an arsenal of texts," a collection of propositions "whose logical implications were to be elicited and reconciled into self-consistent dogma." [40] Abelard began and Aquinas completed the subordination—perhaps enslavement is the better word—of exegesis to theology. The result was that in late medieval teaching and writing, the Bible became buried fathoms deep under layer after layer of theological comment. What a New Testament writer may actually have meant by a word, a phrase, or an image was almost entirely lost in the luxuriant growth of dialectical and dogmatic glosses, while the unity of thought and approach of a whole Gospel or Epistle was obscured by an analysis which inched along worm-like, line-by-line.

How exciting—and perhaps unsettling—it must have been to many in his crowded audience when young Colet got up and began to talk about Paul, the person who wrote the epistles—about the Christians in Corinth to whom he was writing—about the moral and political situation in

Middle Ages, 2nd ed., Oxford, 1952, especially pp. 292 ff., 363; and ROBERT M. GRANT, *The Bible in the Church: A Short History of Interpretation*, New York, 1948, pp. 98–108.
[40] SEEBOHM, *op. cit.*, p. 17; DUHAMEL, *loc. cit.*, p. 496.

Rome—about what Paul was trying to say to these two groups of early Christians, particularly his moral advice —about his tact, his firmness, and his vision of Christ. The hardest effort in all scholarship is to rise from grasp of the minute and disconnected to grasp of the whole. Colet made it clear from the start in both series of lectures that he was concerned about the whole of what St. Paul had to say' in the whole Epistle. "Everything Paul said must be cautiously examined before any opinion is offered about his meaning." [41] "We have tried so far as possible," he concluded the lectures on *Romans*, "with the aid of God's grace, to express Paul's true meaning. How we have succeeded, we hardly know. But we have had the best will to do it." [42]

Colet's interest was personal, moral, and religious, rather than dogmatic or theological. Abelard had taken Romans 5: 12 ("wherefore as by one man sin entered into the world, and death by sin; and so death passed upon all men, for that all have sinned") and used it characteristically as a peg upon which to hang a discussion of the doctrine of original sin. Colet used the passage as a window into Paul's mind, concluding, "Sin is certainly a violent and overwhelming thing; but nothing can resist the magnificent power of sweet and delightful grace, that works softly and marvelously, with a certain secret and wonder-working power." [43] And so over and over he is concerned with three things: Paul himself (with whom Colet had obviously fallen in love, as Petrarch with Cicero), his audience in Corinth or Rome, and the moral and religious import of what he had to say. From a congeries of dialectical propositions, the Epistles are transformed into historical letters with lessons for the present. Scripture has a dual meaning for Colet: historical (what Paul said to the Corinthians) and contem-

---

[41] COLET, *Romans*, p. 145.

[42] *Ibid.*, p. 227.

[43] *Ibid.*, p. 142.

porary (what he says to Colet's generation). His trip to Italy and his study of the Dionysian writings, with their picture of a Church far more simply organized than that of the fifteenth century, combined with earlier experiences to make of Colet a moral reformer, almost a "puritan." In the Oxford lectures, Paul and Colet together have much to say about fifteenth-century evils: simony, ecclesiastical litigation, clerical covetousness, and war. Here were the roots of Colet's later famous sermons as Dean of St. Paul's castigating clerical abuses and advocating a Christian pacifism. Much of Sir Thomas More's firm grasp of the structural character of social evil so evident in *Utopia* comes direct from his friend Colet.[44]

The technique is Jerome's—and Valla's. Grammar and rhetoric have triumphed over dialectic. What Paul said and why he chose to say it the way he did, not how his words relate to a dogmatic proposition, are the center of attention. Colet's "considerations of text and context," writes Duhamel, "involving linguistic, historical, and ethical knowledge were the work of a Renaissance humanist grammarian intent upon the direct meaning of the text he studied, not its dialectical implications."[45] But the spirit is often Augustine's. With all his insight into social evil, Colet never forgets that sin is personal. Paul speaks across the centuries not only to his age but to him, John Colet: "Oh, how dreadful in the sight of God are sins! Oh, how great is man's confusion! Here do I, helpless one, conscious of my sins and blushing at them in secret, cry suddenly and lift up my voice to Thee, most loving God and Father; saying, Impute not unto me my sins!"[46]

It is well not to exaggerate Colet's originality. There are long arid passages in his lectures and expositions of Scrip-

---

[44] LUPTON, *Life*, p. 75.
[45] DUHAMEL, *loc. cit.*, p. 506.
[46] COLET, "Exposition . . . Romans," *Radulphus*, p. 127. On Colet's Au-

ture. There are occasional lapses into mystical interpretation along the order of Pico's *Heptaplus*. His whole work of interpretation rested upon the Vulgate, since he never learned Greek (to his later regret). And what linguistic criticism there is is often clumsy and ill-informed. Lupton remarks on the "singular mixture" in Colet's lectures "of Dionysian mysticism, of scholastic terminology, of 'grammatical' interpretations, and of the outbursts of a deep and genuine conviction, shaking off traditional forms and speaking with an eloquence all its own." [47] But these qualifications do not affect what we have already said, that Colet's Oxford lectures mark something new and creative in the history of Christian scholarship.

Let us try to state as precisely as possible what Colet's conception of his calling was and what he actually accomplished. It seems a reasonable assumption that he returned from his study in Italy convinced that he had found an exciting new way of reading and understanding sacred texts and that he must communicate his findings to as many as could understand what he had to say. He made no public attack on the Schoolmen and their methods—he simply ignored them. He announced no new theological insight (as Luther was to do twenty years later), no new exegetical theory. He put his insight to work, translated his theory into practice. In short, he talked and wrote as directly as he was able to the friends and acquaintances he thought would understand what he was talking about.

gustinianism, see E. F. RICE, JR., "John Colet and the Annihilation of the Natural," *Harvard Theological Review*, XLV (July 1952), 141–163.

[47] LUPTON, *Life*, pp. 86–87. Biblical commentaries of the 14th and 15th centuries had been moving in the direction of Colet's interpretation. They showed a heightened interest in naturalistic detail and secular implications, together with new emphasis on mystical implications. See SMALLEY, *op. cit.*, pp. 359–373.

The concern to communicate was characteristic of the Revival of Learning. In fact, fascination with the whole problem of communication was one of the distinguishing marks of the Revival as a whole. It was embodied particularly in the new reverence among many fifteenth-century scholars for rhetoric. Valla was as interested in rhetoric as in grammar. There was a sense in which all cognition to him was communication.[48] The art of knowing is integrally related to the art of communicating; one test of truth is that it can be articulated, simply, clearly, and persuasively. "Nor is he to be esteemed a true orator," wrote Valla, "who knows how to speak well unless he also has the courage to speak." [49] Along with his pragmatic approach to knowledge went a broad interest in the problem of how men communicate with each other—how Cicero won over his audience, for instance, or how Paul convinced those to whom he wrote. Colet absorbed this interest in communication, both in his treatment of Paul and in his own sense of vocation. But we must remember that the scholars of his generation, at a time when printing was in its infancy, did not think of the written or printed word as the only medium of scholarly communication. The first Englishmen who studied in Italy in the early fifteenth century apparently felt no urge to communicate, no obligation to do anything, in fact, but retire with the manuscripts they brought home with them and continue their study. The next generation —Grocyn, Linacre, and William Latimer—lectured and taught the Greek they had learned, but all shared a dislike for appearing in print which was fashionable among their contemporaries.[50] Colet seems to have shared this distaste

---

[48] DUHAMEL, *loc. cit.*, p. 503, note.
[49] *Treatise on the Donation of Constantine*, ed. COLEMAN, p. 23.
[50] LEWIS EINSTEIN, *The Italian Renaissance in England*, New York, 1902, pp. 16, 34, 37, 38.

for publication. But a scholar communicates through his teaching, his conversation, and his correspondence just as truly as through his printed works, and these were Colet's media.

He lectured first on Corinthians, then on Romans, continuing beyond Chapter XI where he had meant to stop because he was "often and repeatedly asked by certain friends, faithful listeners to my interpretations of Paul, to whom I communicated for friendship's sake what I had written on the foregoing part of the Epistle." [51] There is a letter from him (probably of 1497) which offers precious evidence of how these lectures on Romans were received and how he thought of his office as scholar and teacher:

I had with me yesterday evening... a fellow priest, a good and learned man, both an attentive listener to [my expositions of] St. Paul, and most anxious to gain a nearer acquaintance with the Apostle himself. After chatting for a while by the fireside, he drew forth from his bosom a little book, in which were the epistles of St. Paul, carefully copied in his own handwriting. At this I smiled, and quoted approvingly the words of the Gospel: "Where your treasure is, there will your heart be also." "There is nothing in literature," said he in reply, "that I more love or admire than the writings of St. Paul." And he was polite enough to add, with a touch of flattery, that I had done most to raise that liking of his for the Apostle, by my expositions the previous term. I looked at him and said, "I love you, brother, if you love St. Paul; whom I also, along with you, do singularly love and admire." Then I went on to speak at length on the merits and wisdom and divine character of St. Paul; adding that in his Epistles, and that too in every part of them, there was a marvelous fertility both of matter and knowledge; so that if a man did but carefully note and consider them, he might, if he chose, draw from almost every word of the Apostle thoughts to be admired and marked. Fired as

[51] COLET, *Romans*, p. 175.

it were at the saying, "Then I beg you!" he cried, "draw forth something for me now, while we are sitting at our ease . . . ." [52]

Colet goes on to tell how he accepted the challenge, talking *extempore* about what he saw in the first chapter of Romans while his visitor recorded what he said. In a postscript he asked his correspondent to return the letter to him since it contained "matters of doctrine"; not that his letters were worth preserving, he adds, "but if left behind they might help keep alive some recollection of me."

Here was a scholar, then, who published no nine hundred Theses like Pico, nor felt himself heavy with a dozen books he must publish to the world. Instead he lectured, wrote letters, conversed with students and friends. His third series of lectures at Oxford was on "The Hierarchies of Dionysius." A second and more detailed exposition of the first five chapters of Romans he wrote for the instruction of a young man named Edmund. A commentary on Genesis he put down in letters to a friend named Radulphus. Some of his most interesting insights he argued out in letters to Erasmus. After eight years at Oxford (1496–1504) he became Dean of St. Paul's Cathedral and moved from the life of scholar and teacher to that of preacher and administrator, where he is of less interest to us. His influence was to live on in his friends like Erasmus and More, in his students like those already mentioned or like William Tyndale, the translator of the New Testament, who almost certainly heard him at Oxford. It was not to live in that permanent medium of scholarly communication, the printed book—perhaps because he was a perfectionist, perhaps because he became conscious somewhere along the way that by Humanist standards he wrote badly. Erasmus remarked that he spoke better than he wrote. [53]

---

[52] In LUPTON, *Life*, pp. 90–93.
[53] ERASMUS, *Vitrier and Colet*, p. 39.

Colet was no Humanist in the ordinary sense of the word. He seems never to have felt any guilty love for pagan literature like Jerome or Petrarch. He saw no value in reading the ancient poets and philosophers. In his Oxford lectures he specifically condemned the idea that a man had to study the classics in order to understand Scripture. Truth is understood by grace, grace is procured by prayers, and prayers are heard through devotion and self-denial.[54] Man's natural reason has no autonomous power of arriving at the truth without God's aid. Theology is not a "science" to be attained by reason—this was Aquinas' error, he thought —it is a "wisdom" revealed to faith by the divine illumination.[55] Colet steeped himself in Paul's radical pessimism about the natural man and emerged an Augustinian—almost a "Lutheran," in fact—on the helplessness of the unaided intellect. In his lectures on the Dionysian writings, he showed how much he had absorbed of the Neo-Platonic doctrine that mere learning will never save a man. "Not knowledge, but love, leads to eternal life. . . . Ignorant love has a thousand times more power than cold wisdom." He condemned "indiscriminate erudition," saying that it dulled Christian innocence and simplicity.[56] Probably he was referring to the Schoolmen, but it is not impossible that he was thinking of Pico.

Yet when all is said on the side of Colet's narrow intellectual interests and almost puritanical Christianity (he had absorbed Paul's view of marriage as a mere concession to human infirmity), the fact remains that he was able to direct a penetrating mind and a devout heart into a brief

---

[54] COLET, *I Corinthians*, p. 110.
[55] RICE, "John Colet and the Annihilation of the Natural," *loc. cit.*, pp. 152–161.
[56] COLET, *Two Treatises on the Hierarchies of Dionysius*, ed. J. H. LUPTON, London, 1869, p. 219; ERASMUS, *Vitrier and Colet*, p. 37.

scholarly career of considerable significance. Within the Christian tradition itself, his tastes were not narrow or dogmatic. He read heretical books with attention, says Erasmus, and got more out of them than he did out of orthodox scholastic hair-splitters.[57] His scholarly ideal, even when he failed to live up to it in his own writing, was directness and simplicity. He once read a copy of Reuchlin's *Cabalistica* and wrote Erasmus that he was not really qualified to discuss it, but that as he read, it seemed to him at times that "the wonders were more verbal than real." [58] What came to his mind in commenting on Romans 1: 17 was quite characteristic. He chose to remark on how simple was the Apostles' method of citation when quoting from the Old Testament (in this case, Paul was quoting "The just shall live by faith" from Habakkuk). In contrast, he said, modern theologians and lawyers are so afraid no one will believe them that they pile citation upon citation to show off their erudition.[59]

Christian scholarship to Colet begins in prayer and divine illumination; it concerns itself with the whole of a scriptural writer's thought and his historical surroundings; it moves on from historical analysis to ethical and religious understanding; and it ends in social reform and the deepening of personal piety. Unlike any of the moving spirits of the Revival of Learning in Italy whom we have considered, Colet was able to adapt the historical and philological approach to the reverent study of Scripture and to bring his own Christian piety into fruitful relationship with humanistic scholarship. His example was to have important effects upon the greatest scholar of the age, Erasmus of Rotterdam.

---

[57] ERASMUS, *Vitrier and Colet*, p. 38.
[58] LUPTON, *Colet*, pp. 225–226.
[59] COLET, *Romans*, p. 209.

CHAPTER III

Erasmus

SOME of the questions that faced thoughtful and devoted Christian minds at the close of the fifteenth century—none of them very clearly expressed at the time—were these: How real was the threat to Christian belief implied in the new enthusiasm for pagan antiquity? Could the critical techniques of the New Learning be adapted to Christian uses? Would the application of historical and philological criticism to Christian tradition result in reform or revolution, revival or destruction? To echo the question of Tertullian with which we began this study, we might say that men were wondering once more what Athens had to do with Jerusalem. Would the Humanists of the New Athens help build a New Jerusalem or would they deliver the *coup de grâce* to the Old?

We have seen that John Colet was able to travel to the New Athens (in Italy) and return fired with the call to build the New Jerusalem (in England). In him we can begin to see the silhouette of a new kind of Christian scholar, convinced of the importance of the original sources, endowed with a fresh sense of historical perspective, disillusioned with scholastic philosophy, yet at the same time warmly committed to preaching Christ and to reforming ecclesiastical abuses. Colet's strength was in his single-mindedness, the integrity of his character, and the depth of his faith. As a scholar, he had his weaknesses. He had only a vague grasp of the importance of a thorough re-examination of the whole Christian tradition as it had been shaped by medieval scholars. He had almost no vision of the need to relate Christian belief to a rediscovered pagan antiquity. He had most of the scholar's instincts but no desire to publish and no sense of the importance to Christendom of the invention of printing just before his birth. He knew the importance of getting back to the sources, but he knew no Greek and so could not thrust aside the final veil between himself and the mind of his beloved Paul.

Twenty years after Colet began to lecture on St. Paul's Epistles at Oxford the educated world of Europe rang not with his name but with that of his friend, Erasmus of Rotterdam. It was Erasmus, not Colet, who became known as the greatest scholar of his age, the Christian Humanist *par excellence* who loved both Socrates and Jesus, both Plato and Paul, with almost equal enthusiasm, who caught the vision of a Christendom restored to sanity and devotion through the labors of Christian men of learning, and exhausted his body, his mind—yes, even his spirit—in the vain but heroic effort to save his generation through sheer scholarship. But it was Colet more than any other human being who was the source of Erasmus' vision and sense of calling.[1]

---

[1] On Colet's influence upon Erasmus see F. SEEBOHM, *The Oxford Reformers*, London, Everyman, 1914, pp. 69, 99 ff., 294, and *passim;*

The two were almost the same age (about thirty-two) when they first met at Oxford in 1499. Erasmus was perhaps a few months younger, but Colet was by far the more mature. The Erasmus who arrived from Paris in the fall of that year for his first visit to England was an accomplished classical scholar of conventional Christian beliefs who had become a monk some ten years earlier after the death of his parents, had taken badly to the life of the cloister, and had managed to get permission to study for a doctor's degree at the University of Paris. Somewhere very early in his boyhood he had acquired a taste for Latin literature, perhaps from his father (who had traveled in Italy), perhaps at the school of the Brethren of the Common Life at Deventer. He was an omnivorous reader, and in spite of the Philistine attitude of most of his brethren in the monastery at Steyn, he found a few kindred spirits there and was able to indulge his love for reading and writing. Netherlanders before him, like Englishmen before Colet,

J. H. LUPTON, *Life of John Colet*, London, 1887, pp. 96–101, 109–113, and *passim;* J. B. PINEAU, *Erasme: Sa pensée religieuse*, Paris, 1924, pp. 89–100; W. SCHWARZ, *Principles and Problems of Biblical Translation*, Cambridge University, 1955, pp. 110, 111, 114, 120. The view of these writers that Erasmus was strongly, if not decisively, influenced by his contact with Colet is contested, rather unconvincingly, by A. HYMA, "Erasmus and the Oxford Reformers, 1493–1503," *Nederlandsch Archief voor Kerkgeschiedenis*, XXV (1932), N.S., pp. 69–92, 97–134. Little is added to the argument in the same author's continuation, "1503–1519," *loc. cit.*, XXXVIII (1952), pp. 65–85. E. F. RICE, JR., "John Colet and the Annihilation of the Natural," *Harvard Theological Review*, XLV (July 1952), pp. 141–163, properly emphasizes the great differences between Colet, the Augustinian, and Erasmus, the Humanist, and suggests that Erasmus was more influenced by the image of Colet which he created in 1521 after the latter's death than he was by the real Colet of the Oxford Lectures. For purposes of the present study, Erasmus' own feelings about Colet as revealed by his correspondence are crucial. My own interpretation of this evidence will appear in what follows.

had visited Italy and brought back enthusiasm for the work of the Italian Humanists, particularly Lorenzo Valla. Erasmus' own particular favorites, ancient and modern, were Lucian, Jerome, and Valla.

There is precious little piety in his early letters and writings, but also no consciousness whatever of a breach with Christian teachings or practice. The dominant note is a naive secularism, combined with wholehearted acceptance of Christian ethics. There is no conflict in conscience between his devotion to pagan literature and his loyalty to Christ. The classics, he argues (following well-beaten apologetic paths), are shot through with moral precepts and ethical allegories useful to a Christian life; and conversely, Christian belief is useful to a life of virtue. In other words, he moralizes antiquity and strips Christianity to a great extent of its miraculous and mystical elements. He then finds that he can live very comfortably with an ideal compounded of classical moderation and Christian benevolence. He is a monk of very unmonkish tastes, on leave from his monastery to study theology under a scholastic method which he despises. He is apt to lump most monks and Schoolmen together as "barbarians," in typical Humanist fashion. But he does not attack monasticism or Scholasticism as such. He simply says the monastic life is not for persons of a delicate constitution like himself, and that philosophy is an excellent thing "if used moderately." [2]

But this is not the whole story. There were unseen possibilities in this young Dutch scholar who turned up at Oxford in 1499. He was a sensitive person who had known

---

[2] E. F. RICE, JR., "Erasmus and the Religious Tradition, 1495–1499," *Journal of the History of Ideas*, XI (Oct. 1950), 387–411, particularly 404. Also J. HUIZINGA, *Erasmus of Rotterdam*, London, Phaidon Press, 1952, chaps. I–III; P. S. ALLEN, *The Age of Erasmus*, Oxford, 1914, chaps. I–IV; and SCHWARZ, *op. cit.*, pp. 95–107.

suffering. His illegitimate birth always weighed on him, and he had been rebuffed in his one unguarded bid for friendship with a fellow monk at Steyn because he demanded too much. He was therefore sensitive to others' needs—and still more sensitive to others' opinions. He had an extraordinarily subtle mind and an unrivalled grasp of the Latin language, the *lingua franca* of the age. He had energy, enthusiasm, a keen wit, and a store of common sense. And finally, his instincts were Christian. Something of the pietistic teaching of the Brethren of the Common Life had struck its root in him, ready to blossom under the proper conditions. The one thing this Erasmus had never yet experienced was to meet a thoroughly devoted Christian with a first-rate mind and scholarly tastes something like his own.

This is why his meeting with Colet was so important. It was an interesting contrast: on the one side, brilliance, wit, and an unrivalled literary talent, without clear direction or purpose; on the other, "that unequalled power which comes from a single eye, a pure heart, and an undivided purpose." [3] There was no Road to Damascus in Erasmus' life, no bitter inner struggle resulting in violent crisis and conversion. All his life Erasmus was being converted, and the process was never quite completed. He matured slowly, the experiences and personal influences of one stage of his life often bearing fruit only months or years later. But certainly the two or three months at Oxford, probably in almost daily contact with Colet, were the crucial period. Colet showed him the possibilities of a career devoted to Christian scholarship and excited him enough to make him ponder what such a career would involve. Characteristically, there was no Vision, no Voice from on high, only a series of leisurely arguments about the interpretation of Scripture with a friend just as

---

[3] LUPTON, *Colet*, p. 109.

knowledgeable as Erasmus himself in scholastic and humanistic learning—and far more knowledgeable in what it meant to be a Christian.

On one occasion, a dinner-party at which Colet presided, the question came up why Cain's sacrifice was unacceptable to God. Colet was serious and animated. To Erasmus he seemed "clothed with a dignity and majesty more than human." He maintained that Cain had offended God by so distrusting God's bounty and overvaluing his own exertions as to till the soil, and he carried the argument against Erasmus and another guest. The talk became too long and too serious for Erasmus, and he finally told a story—an outrageously amusing tale which he concocted on the spur of the moment. Cain, he said, heard that the grain grew as high as alders in Paradise and set out to wheedle a few seeds out of the Angel on guard duty at the gates. He told the Angel a few grains would never be missed, so long as he didn't meddle with the apples. After all, God was treating the Angel shabbily to begin with, he said, by chaining him to a job that men were now training watch-dogs to handle on earth. Earth is a pretty nice spot, he added, in case the Angel wanted to move. Cain's arguments prevailed. He got the seed, sowed it, and it multiplied. Then God found out, destroyed Cain's crop, and appropriately imprisoned the derelict Angel in a human body. The classical poet in Erasmus was still stronger, obviously, than the theologian.[4]

In time, however, Colet managed to impress Erasmus

---

[4] P. S. and H. M. ALLEN, *Opus Epistolarum Des. Erasmi Roterodami*, Oxford, 1906–47 (hereafter cited as ALLEN), Vol. I, Epistle 116; trans. in F. M. NICHOLS, *The Epistles of Erasmus*, London, 1901–18 (hereafter cited as NICHOLS), Vol. I, Epistle 105. I see no good reason for placing this incident "in the latter part of Erasmus' visit" to Oxford, as Allen does.

with the seriousness and importance of theological and exegetical problems. They both agreed in their dislike of scholastic method, but Colet had thought more deeply into the matter. One day Erasmus praised Aquinas as the ablest of the Schoolmen. Colet looked at him sharply to make sure he was in earnest, then blazed forth: "Why do you praise to me a man who, had he not had so much arrogance, would never have defined everything in such a rash and supercilious way, and who, had he not had a worldly spirit, would never have contaminated the teaching of Christ with his profane philosophy?" This was strong language, almost "Lutheran" in its intensity. Erasmus' Humanist friends sneered at Scholasticism for its barbarous style and its practical uselessness. But here was a man whose *religious* feelings were outraged by the intellectual arrogance of the whole scholastic enterprise. Erasmus was impressed.[5]

The conversation that stirred him to write his first essay in biblical interpretation, however, was on the subject of Christ's agony in the Garden of Gethsemane and how to explain it. Erasmus, Humanist that he was, saw in the agony a moment of fear and weakness in Jesus as man, confronted by the awful certainty of his death. Colet could not believe that Christ had quailed when so many lesser martyrs had faced death without flinching. He argued (follow-

---

[5] ALLEN, IV, Ep. 1211, p. 520; ERASMUS, *Lives of Vitrier and Colet*, trans. J. H. LUPTON, p. 33. Cf. SEEBOHM, *op. cit.*, pp. 61–67. I assume that this incident took place during Erasmus' first visit with Colet in 1499, although he does not say so. Erasmus was impressed enough to remember the incident but not enough to be convinced by Colet. In his note on Romans 1:4 in the *New Testament* he wrote of Aquinas: "There is not one of the scholastic theologians who has equal industry, who has a more wholesome character, who has more solid learning .... Think of what that master mind could have achieved if he only had had Greek and Hebrew." E. L. SURTZ, "The Oxford Reformers and Scholasticism," *Studies in Philology*, XLVII (1950), p. 550.

ing Jerome) that Jesus was momentarily overwhelmed with pity for the Jews, who were to be guilty of his death. Erasmus was not convinced. He sat down and wrote out his argument in two brief essays. "These," he wrote Colet, "are the first attempts of a novice in theology. They show my application, if not my skill." He was plainly more in earnest than he had been in the problem of Cain, but he still gave the impression of toying with new ideas, while Colet (in the one reply that has survived) was clearly writing from deep conviction. He was sure that there could be no human flaw in his Saviour.[6]

After a month or so the two men came to know each other fairly well. Somewhere along the way their growing friendship must have reached a kind of crisis: either it would ripen into intimate mutual understanding and the sense of standing enlisted in a common cause, or it would wither because of the temperamental differences between the two. Colet must have felt a little like Jesus confronted with the rich young ruler. Here (in Erasmus' case) was a brilliant possible convert to the cause of Christian scholarship. Should he risk his friendship in order to gain his support? Colet decided to take the risk. He wrote Erasmus what was probably the most important letter Erasmus ever received. It reflected what must have been numerous conversations between the two. The letter is lost, but we know something of what it said from Erasmus' reply.[7]

Colet seems to have put squarely up to Erasmus the decision which would affect the whole future course of his life: Was he going to waste his extraordinary talents by de-

---

[6] ALLEN, I, Eps. 109, 110, 111; LUPTON, *Colet*, pp. 101–108; J. B. PINEAU, *Erasme: sa pensée religieuse*, Paris, 1924, pp. 97–100. Calvin, incidentally, agreed with Erasmus. *Institutes* II, 16, 12.

[7] ALLEN, I, Ep. 108; NICHOLS, I, Ep. 108. Cf. LUPTON, *Colet*, pp. 109–113; PINEAU, *op. cit.*, pp. 91–97; SCHWARZ, *op. cit.*, pp. 114–120.

voting his life to secular Poetry and Rhetoric, as he apparently intended, or would he immediately join Colet in his battle with the sophists and obscurantists who were hiding knowledge of the Gospel, settle down at Oxford, and perhaps start right in to lecture on Moses or Isaiah as Colet was lecturing on Paul? It was a strong letter. According to Erasmus, it contained pointed admonitions and reproaches. Somewhere in it Colet said flatly he was disappointed in Erasmus. But it was still the letter of a friend.

Erasmus replied that Colet was expecting too much of him. The battle with the obscurantists took courage, like Colet's, and Erasmus said he did not have it although he agreed that the battle had to be fought. Furthermore, he didn't yet have the intellectual equipment. "With what countenance shall I teach what I have never learned? How am I to warm the coldness of others while I am shivering myself?" he asked. If he had disappointed Colet, it was because Colet had overestimated him. He never meant to devote himself to Poetry and Rhetoric. These were beneath his purpose now just as sacred studies were still beyond his strength. But he insisted he was on Colet's side. For the time being, he promised his "earnest encouragement and sympathy." "And further when I am conscious of the proper strength, I will put myself on your side and will make an earnest, if not an effective, effort in defence of theology."

We may take this either as a piece of understandable pusillanimity or as a bit of honest and penetrating self-analysis. Probably there was something of both in it. The important thing was that Erasmus was half-committing himself to his life's work and that he was correctly measuring its magnitude against his own stature. He knew himself better than Colet did. He must already have had a vague notion that really to reshape the Christian tradition and relate it to the best in classical culture was a task requiring the broadest and deepest kind of intellectual preparation. We know that he left England determined to learn Greek. Whether this was merely so that he might read Greek literature in the original, as a recent writer maintains, or whether he already saw the relevance of Greek to biblical studies, is not altogether clear.[8] Others whom he met in England—William Grocyn and Thomas Linacre, for example—knew Greek even if Colet did not. We have only an imperfect record in his letters of all his conversations with these friends, and it seems possible that the significance of Greek for biblical study, which he realized quite clearly a year or two later, was suggested to him in England. It is even possible that when he asked Colet how he could teach what he had never learned, he was subtly reproaching his friend for lecturing on St. Paul with no knowledge of Greek. In any case, he may have learned something from Colet's weakness as well as from his strength.

Erasmus left England for Paris in January 1500. During the next few years his vocation became increasingly clear to him: to apply the best humanistic scholarship of his day to the key documents of the Christian faith, with a view to cleansing and purifying the whole religious tradition. These were the hardest years of his life. He was terribly sensi-

---

[8] W. SCHWARZ, *Principles and Problems of Biblical Translation*, Cambridge University Press, 1955, pp. 120–121, argues that because Colet did not see the importance of the original Hebrew and Greek texts, it is "very unlikely that in 1499 Erasmus's wish to learn Greek was connected with biblical studies .... There is no evidence that while in England he fully comprehended the significance of Greek for theological studies .... How could he judge of the value of Greek before he knew the language and before he himself had found out the discrepancies between the Latin text of the Vulgate and the Greek Bible? Nobody was able to assist him in arriving at this idea which was contrary to all tradition." The argument is persuasive but not altogether conclusive. See below.

tive to physical discomforts, but during these years of poverty and illness his determination to gain the intellectual weapons he needed never flagged. It was no easy task to learn Greek in a day when there were almost no dictionaries, manuscripts were scarce and expensive, and teachers hard to come by. Apparently he had a teacher for a time —"and a thorough Greek he is," Erasmus reported, "always hungry, and charging an exorbitant price for his lessons." But the job depended mostly on his own efforts. He knew he was old for the task but told himself it was better late than never. Latin learning was "crippled and imperfect without Greek." "We have in Latin at best some small streams and turbid pools, while they have the clearest springs and rivers flowing with gold." To touch theology without a knowledge of Greek was sheerest madness, he thought. The Council of Vienne (1311–12) had piously commanded the teaching of Hebrew, Greek, and Latin at the chief universities of Christendom, but he noted that the decree had not been carried out. "We cannot be anything in any kind of literature without Greek. For it is one thing to guess and another thing to judge; one thing to believe your own eyes, another thing to believe other people's." And so Erasmus stuck at it until he had mastered the language. His simultaneous attempt to learn Hebrew failed. He gave it up because of his age and because of "the insufficiency of the human mind to master a multitude of subjects." [9]

There were no grants from governments or fellowships from private foundations in 1500, and so a scholar like Erasmus who wanted to prepare himself for an ambitious scholarly career in his mid-thirties had to depend upon his wealthy friends for backing. His begging letters of these

---

[9] ALLEN, I, Ep. 149; NICHOLS, I, Ep. 143. ALLEN, I, Ep. 181; NICHOLS, I, Ep. 180.

years are not pleasant reading. He calls upon his friend James Batt to approach the Lady of Veere and not take no for an answer. Tell her, he says, that her other protégés "preach obscure sermons; I write what will live forever; they, with their ignorant rubbish, are heard in one or two churches; my books will be read in every country in the world. . . . You know your old ways of lying profusely in praise of your Erasmus." In the next breath he says he is going blind by reading, like St. Jerome; perhaps the Lady can be persuaded to send him "some sapphire or other gem that has the power of strengthening the eyesight." "A great dearth of books; leisure none; health infirm. Go and try yourself to write books in such circumstances," he complains.[10]

In all this exaggeration, prevarication, and distressing humiliation, there was a kernel of integrity. There is always an irreducible egotism in most scholarship. Unless the scholar believes passionately in what he is doing, no matter how far off the results or remote the audience or infinitesimal the apparent rewards, the job will never get done—or certainly will not be well done. Others had had to sacrifice comfort, family, and pleasure to finish a work of scholarship; Erasmus had also to sacrifice his self-respect. But there was no mistaking his sincerity of purpose. "It is incredible how my heart burns to bring all my poor products of the midnight oil to completion and at the same time to attain some moderate capacity in Greek," he writes a year after leaving England; "I should then devote myself entirely to the study of Sacred Literature, as for some time I have longed to do." The time is ripe, he says, to attack the obscurantists as he has long meant to do, and he hopes for three more years of health in which to carry out the on-

---

[10] ALLEN, I, Ep. 139; NICHOLS, I, Ep. 139.

slaught. "My whole soul is bent on acquiring the most perfect learning and hence I have a supreme disregard for learning of a trivial kind. . . . I had rather wait long for a solid reputation than acquire at an early age one not likely to last. . . . There shall be no want of industry or courage on my part." [11]

A good deal has been written in disparagement of Erasmus' courage. Too little has been said about the remarkable fortitude and singleness of purpose he displayed in these hard years before he became famous. And it has too seldom been remarked that in his most difficult years he held before himself an ideal of significant scholarship, as contrasted with trivial research or premature publication, which might well serve any century.

Between 1500 and 1505, while he was living sometimes in France, sometimes in the Netherlands, learning Greek and eking out a living by doing literary hack-work, publishing his *Adages,* and begging from wealthy patrons, the general goal of devoting himself to sacred studies began to take on concrete form.[12] He had talked vaguely about such a goal several times even before his visit to England but now the objective took definite shape for the first time as he gradually discovered the particular projects to which he wished to give himself.

The first was editing St. Jerome. Jerome's Letters had long been favorite reading with him. Early in his life he had copied out every one of them with his own hand. Anyone who reads them, he wrote while still in the monastery at Steyn, would agree "that dullness is not sanctity, nor elegance of language, impiety." He particularly liked

---

[11] ALLEN, I, Ep. 138; NICHOLS, I, Ep. 132. ALLEN, I, Ep. 139; NICHOLS, I, Ep. 139.
[12] On the slow development of Erasmus' sense of vocation during these years, see SCHWARZ, *op. cit.*, pp. 120–138, 141, 161.

Jerome's use of Deuteronomy's injunctions about shaving a captive woman as a symbol of the Christian's use of pagan literature. It was a fine javelin to throw at the clerical "Barbarians" who despised secular culture, he thought. Perhaps (as P. S. Allen suggests) the fact that Colet based himself on Jerome in arguing his position on Christ's Agony had induced Erasmus to reread his favorite author. At any rate, we learn that it was his aim, barely a year after leaving Oxford, to edit and publish Jerome's Epistles, restoring the original Greek passages which had been dropped out during intervening centuries. "The restoration of the works of St. Jerome and the revival of true Theology": this was his "great design" at the end of 1500.[13] The two parts of the design were closely linked in his mind. To restore the man who was himself the restorer of the Scriptures would be to overthrow the "Barbarians," to get back to the best early interpretation, and to restore the fruitful interaction of classical learning and Christian faith represented by Jerome himself.

A second object of study appeared the next year and began to move toward the center of his attention. This was the New Testament. Colet had invited him to lecture at Oxford on the Old Testament, but Colet's own example in lecturing on St. Paul was apparently more persuasive than his advice. At any rate, in the fall of 1501 his friend, Jacques Vitrier, got Erasmus interested in studying Paul's Epistles, and about the same time he brought his *Handbook of a Christian Soldier* to a close with these words: "Make the Prophets, Christ, and the Apostles your friends. Above all, choose Paul.... For long I have been laboring over a commentary upon him.... I hope to disarm some critics who

---

[13] ALLEN, I, Ep. 22; NICHOLS, I, Ep. 29. ALLEN, I, Ep. 139, l. 42; NICHOLS, I, Ep. 139. ALLEN, I, Ep. 141; NICHOLS, I, Ep. 134. Cf. ALLEN, *The Age of Erasmus*, Oxford, 1914, p. 138.

think it is the highest religion to know nothing of good learning. It was not for empty fame or childish pleasure that in my youth I grasped at the polite literature of the ancients, and by late hours gained some slight mastery of Greek and Latin. It has long been my cherished wish to cleanse the Lord's temple of barbarous ignorance, and to adorn it with treasures brought from afar, such as may kindle in generous hearts a warm love for the Scriptures." [14] How like—and how unlike—this thought of a planned intellectual development is to Augustine's reflections on his own evolution. Erasmus exaggerates the planning and says he was the planner; Augustine ascribes his intellectual Odyssey to God's providence.

In December 1504, five years after leaving Oxford, Erasmus wrote Colet that his purpose was settled.[15] "I cannot tell you, most excellent Colet," he said, "how eagerly I am pursuing sacred literature and how I chafe at every hindrance or delay." He has returned to Paris from Louvain to free himself from entanglements. "Then in freedom and with all my heart I shall tackle the divine studies to which I intend to devote the rest of my life." The four rolls which he had written on Paul's epistle to the Romans had been left unfinished, he says, because he was constantly hampered by his lack of Greek, but this had now been remedied. Saying he had not heard from Colet for "several years," he enclosed copies of his recent writings, but for some reason not clear now he did not mention the most exciting event of the past summer. While rummaging

---

[14] *Desiderii Erasmi Roterodami Opera Omnia*, ed. J. CLERICUS, Lugduni Batavorum, 1703–6, Vol. V, column 66B (hereafter cited as *Opera, LB*); trans. in P. S. ALLEN, *Erasmus: Lectures and Wayfaring Sketches*, Oxford, Clarendon Press, 1934, pp. 42–43. Cf. ALLEN, I, Ep. 164, p. 375.

[15] ALLEN, I, Ep. 181; NICHOLS, I, Ep. 180.

through a monastic library near Louvain—no more delightful sport, he later remarked—he had come upon a copy of Lorenzo Valla's *Notes on the New Testament.* He had long admired Valla, chiefly for his linguistic studies. The *Notes* were new to him and he must have thrilled to their discovery. Somehow he managed to take the manuscript with him to Paris (such things were easier then) and there he found a publisher in the spring of 1505.

Erasmus presented Valla's *Notes* to the public in a very significant preface.[16] In this preface three Christian Humanists met and joined hands across the centuries: Jerome, Valla, and Erasmus. The result was a ringing declaration of independence by Grammar (Philology) over against Theology. The theologians would raise "a most odious outcry," Erasmus was sure, against "this grammarian," Valla, for meddling with Scripture although he had no theological degree. (Erasmus knew, but did not say, that he was in the same case.) They will say that interpretation depends upon the influence of the Holy Spirit, not upon knowledge of the original languages of the Scriptures. But they should remember Jerome's dictum that "it is one thing to be a prophet, and another to be a translator." "Shall we ascribe to the Holy Spirit the errors which we ourselves make" because of linguistic ignorance?, he asks. They will say that Valla has no respect for Jerome's Latin because he compares it with the Greek. But Jerome only emended an earlier Latin translation, he did not start from the Greek; furthermore, errors have multiplied as the years have rolled by; and now corruption has been "made easier than ever by printing, which propagates a single error in a thousand

---

[16] Reprinted in *Laurentii Vallae Opera,* Basel, 1540, pp. 803–875. Erasmus' Preface in ALLEN, I, Ep. 182; NICHOLS, I, Ep. 182. This Preface is echoed in REUCHLIN's *De Rudimentis Hebraicis,* published in 1506. See SCHWARZ, *op. cit.,* p. 137.

copies at once." They will say that the ancient scholars have already brought out every hidden meaning in Scripture and said everything there is to be said, but "I had rather see with my own eyes than with those of others," says Erasmus; and there is still much to be said by each new generation. There is simply no substitute for going to the sources and reading them for yourself, he concludes. Theology is ultimately dependent upon her handmaiden, Grammar. Even a theologian should not write about Holy Writ unless he knows the language in which it was originally written.

Here was Erasmus' Inaugural Lecture as Professor-at-large to Christendom. All his basic principles were here, explicit or implicit: go to the sources because they are sounder and purer than the commentaries; theology must be based upon a sound linguistic and historical understanding of Scripture; the Scriptural text must not be twisted to suit the needs of Theology; the linguist and historian have as good a right as the theologian to the title of Christian scholar. This was a platform upon which Jerome, Valla, and Erasmus—different as they were—could all stand.

It took Erasmus ten more years to complete his work on Jerome and the New Testament. In the winter of 1505–6 he was back in England. There, fired by Valla's example and probably encouraged by Colet, he made a new Latin translation of most of the New Testament from some Latin and Greek manuscripts that Colet gathered for him.[17] The next three years he was in Italy (1506–9), then he was back in England for five more years (1509–14) except for brief intervals. At Cambridge he lectured on Jerome and worked on Greek manuscripts of the New Testament. By 1514 he was ready and anxious to publish. "During the

---

[17] ALLEN, *Erasmus*, pp. 70–71. ALLEN, *Age of Erasmus*, p. 140. PRE-SERVED SMITH, *Erasmus*, New York and London, 1923, pp. 186–187.

last two years," he wrote, "apart from much else, I have emended the letters of Jerome.... I have corrected the whole of the New Testament from collations of the Greek and ancient manuscripts, and have annotated more than a thousand passages, not without some benefit to theologians. I have begun commentaries on the Epistles of St. Paul, which I shall complete when I have published these. For I have resolved to live and die in the study of the Scriptures. I make these my work and my leisure. Men of consequence say that I can do what others cannot in this field." [18]

As so often with sixteenth-century scholarship, the rest of the story concerns the printer as much as the scholar. The Basel firm of Amorbach and Froben had a project under way to publish the works of the early Fathers, including Jerome. (Rome had been printing the Latin classics, Aldus at Venice was doing the Greeks, Germany the Schoolmen.) Printing had made the production of what we call "standard editions" possible for the first time in the history of scholarship. The need of the day, as Allen has pointed out, was to get out standard editions of the great authors—not perfect editions, but printed texts which scholars everywhere could use as the groundwork for further collation and criticism.[19] Erasmus sensed the enormous significance of printing, as his remark already quoted about multiplying errors in the Vulgate suggests. Others he knew like Colet might be content to lecture; Erasmus had almost a compulsion to publish. He had already had the excite-

---

[18] To Servatius Roger, 8 July 1514, ALLEN, I, Ep. 296, p. 570; trans. by BARBARA FLOWER in J. HUIZINGA, *Erasmus*, Phaidon Press, p. 216. Used by permission. On Erasmus' paraphrases, see ALLEN, *Erasmus*, pp. 60–71; and ALLEN, III, Ep. 710.

[19] ALLEN, *Age of Erasmus*, pp. 146–162. ALLEN, *Erasmus*, Chap. II (a brilliant sketch of "Erasmus' Services to Learning").

ment of working with Aldus in Venice, and in the summer
of 1514 he began his long and fruitful association with
John Froben at Basel.

Erasmus' *New Testament*—the first printed Greek text
to reach the public, with introduction, copious notes, and a
new Latin translation—appeared in March 1516. Froben's
nine-volume edition of Jerome—four volumes devoted to
Erasmus' edition of the Epistles—came out the following
fall. (It was the same year that his friend Sir Thomas
More published *Utopia*.) Next year Erasmus published a
paraphrase of Paul's Epistle to the Romans. The long years
of exhausting labor had begun to bear fruit. The *New
Testament* was to go through five editions before his death
twenty years later (1536). The editor of Jerome went on
later to edit Augustine, Ambrose, Origen, and others of
the Fathers. These were his solidest contributions to scholarship. Meanwhile he made the discovery that paraphrase
—something between translation and commentary, informal,
informative, yet close to the text—was his *forte*. And so he
wrote paraphrases of the rest of the Gospels and Epistles.
They were soon translated into German, French, and English, and attained enormous popularity.

By 1516 Erasmus had found his calling, produced his
two most important works of scholarship, and reached the
height of his intellectual powers and moral prestige. There
was something exciting about the atmosphere of Christendom early in 1517: "All over the world, as if on a given
signal," he wrote, "splendid talents are stirring and awakening and conspiring together to revive the best learning.
For what else is this but a conspiracy, when all these great
scholars from different lands share out the work among
themselves and set about this noble task." Erasmus was
proud of his "humble share" in the work. The medieval
theologians were about done for, he thought. His only

fear was that "under cover of the rebirth of ancient learning paganism may seek to rear its head." But he hoped "that the simplicity and purity of Christ [may] penetrate deeply into the minds of men" and believed that this would happen "if with the help provided by the three languages we exercise our minds in the actual sources." [20] To slay the monsters of Scholasticism and superstition with the sword of a Christianized Humanism—to revive the original purity of the Christian religion by leading his generation back to Galilee through study of the earliest written sources—this was Erasmus' vocation.

The years immediately following the appearance of his *New Testament,* in fact, marked the moment of most enraptured hope among a few in Europe that the deep-rooted evils of the day were about to yield before the onslaught of a little company of devoted and enlightened Christian scholars. In some cases this hope can be traced to the contagion of Erasmus' enthusiasm. But just as often it seems to be a parallel but independent phenomenon in many men of learning scattered all over Europe. We can cite only two examples here.

Sir Thomas More, who was Erasmus' close friend, was as delighted as Colet with Erasmus' *New Testament.* In the spring of 1518 he wrote a famous letter to the Vice-Chancellor, Proctors, and Faculty of the University of Oxford defending Greek learning against its "Trojan" attackers. "As to the question of humanistic education being secular," More wrote, "no one has ever claimed that a man needed Greek and Latin, or indeed any education, in order to be saved. Still this education which he calls secular does train the soul in virtue.... There are some who through knowledge of things natural construct a ladder by which

---

[20] ALLEN, II, Ep. 541, trans. by BARBARA FLOWER in J. HUIZINGA, *Erasmus,* Phaidon Press, pp. 218–221. Used by permission.

to rise to the contemplation of things supernatural; they build a path to Theology through Philosophy and the Liberal Arts ... ; they adorn the Queen of Heaven with the spoils of the Egyptians. ... I don't see how [Theology can be studied] without some knowledge of languages, whether Hebrew or Greek or Latin. ... The New Testament is in Greek. ... Not half of Greek learning has yet been made available to the West; and, however good the translations have been, the text of the original still remains a surer and more convincing presentation." [21] More's letter obviously owed much to Augustine's classic defense of secular studies as a foundation for theological work in his *Christian Instruction*. But it also owed much to Erasmus, who had actually lived out Augustine's doctrine in More's own day.

In contrast, the German Mutianus Rufus, or Mutian, who taught at the University of Erfurt, was a scholar not directly influenced by Erasmus, yet one who went through an analogous sort of development. Like Erasmus, he was an enthusiastic student of the classics in his youth, with great faith in learning. In a satirical tract on religious ceremonies which he wrote, the following exchange takes place: "Some ... wrinkled their brows and said, 'Who will absolve you wicked Christians?' 'Studies,' I answered, 'and knowledge.' " However serious he was in this passage, this was the platform of Christian Humanism. Like Colet, Mutian was afraid of publication, perhaps because he was dubious

---

[21] Text in E. F. ROGERS, ed., *The Correspondence of Sir Thomas More*, Princeton, 1947, pp. 112–120; trans. T. S. K. SCOTT-CRAIG, in *Renaissance News*, I (1948), pp. 17–24. CONYERS READ notes that the English Reformation was "an academic affair in its origins," springing from that little group of "Grecians," followers of Erasmus, who met in St. John's College, Cambridge, which was founded by Erasmus' friend, Bishop Fisher. *Social and Political Forces in the English Reformation*, Houston, 1953, p. 22.

about his own ideas and fearful of their effect. He had a "striking intellectual affinity" with Erasmus in his fondness for Jerome, his emphasis on getting back to the sources, and his conviction that Christianity was a way of life rather than a set of beliefs or ceremonies. In 1514 he experienced some sort of religious awakening, and thereafter his faith in learning became more cautious: "The peasant knows many things which the philosopher does not know," he wrote.[22] But his career is enough to suggest that Erasmus was not alone on the road which he was traveling during the years immediately after 1516.

We are now in a position to inquire somewhat more closely into what was most characteristic and distinctive of Erasmus as a Christian scholar.

The first thing that strikes anyone who comes to know him even slightly is his enormous respect for learning, for good scholarship, for sheer intellectual grasp. All his life he felt he was fighting the monster of ignorance. He was persuaded that truth is strong and compelling and seductive, in spite of the attempts of the "Barbarians" to obscure it. Furthermore, he would say, you can know the truth when you see it because it is always simple and clear. If you come upon complexity and contradiction, you have found a human perversion of the truth, not the truth itself. It may take a great deal of effort and nocturnal lucubrations (a favorite word of Erasmus), but the truth can be learned if you acquire the proper intellectual implements and go to the sources to dig it out. The best-known example of the results of this technique was Erasmus' translation of John the Baptist's cry in the wilderness: "Repent, the Kingdom of Heaven is at hand" (Matthew 3:2; cf. Romans 2:4). Erasmus saw that the Vulgate's *poenitentiam agite,* "do penance," obscured the root-meaning of the Greek: "return

[22] Lewis W. Spitz, "The Conflict of Ideals in Mutianus Rufus," *Journal of the Warburg and Courtauld Institutes,* XVI (1953), 121–143.

to your right mind." This bit of philological research was to play an important part in shaping Luther's new understanding of the meaning of penance and penitence in 1518.

Early in his life Erasmus wrote a friend, "Always remember Pliny's maxim: all time is lost which you do not devote to study." At the close of his life he wrote, "They tell me that if I am to live I must give up all writing, indeed study of any sort. But life at such a price is no life." [23] To Erasmus, study was the most exciting, the most rewarding, the most satisfying thing in life. One of the most delightful of his Colloquies is a conversation between an ignorant Abbot and a well-read Woman. (Erasmus was always standing up for women and running down monks.) "I should be loath, I do assure you," says the Abbot, "to have my monks over-bookish. . . . It teaches 'em to chop logic and makes 'em undutiful. You shall have them expostulating presently, appealing to Peter and Paul. . . ." "But," says the Woman, "I hope you would not have them do anything that clashes with Peter and Paul though." "Clash or not clash," replies the Abbot, "I do not much trouble my head about their doctrine; but I do naturally hate a fellow that will have the last word and reply upon his Superior." [24] Cast in more serious language, the same thought runs through the prefaces to Erasmus' *New Testament:* ignorance of Hebrew, Greek, and Latin, the languages of Scripture, is something to be ashamed of, not to be proud of as some theological Barbarians maintain; the "philosophy of Christ" *can* be learned if you go to the sources; "only be teachable . . . ." [25]

---

[23] ALLEN, I, Ep. 56; NICHOLS, I, Ep. 46. ALLEN, *Erasmus*, p. 54.

[24] *Twenty Two Select Colloquies out of Erasmus,* ed. ROGER L'ESTRANGE, London, 1711, p. 229.

[25] "Tantum esto docilis," Paraclesis, *Opera, LB,* V, 140A. There is a French translation of the Paraclesis in PIERRE MESNARD, "La Paraclésis d'Erasme," *Bibliothèque d'humanisme et renaissance,* XIII (1951), 26–42. Eng. trans. of excerpts in SEEBOHM, *op. cit.,* pp. 202–206.

Our second observation is that on closer inspection it is a particular kind of scholarship, a particular approach to learning, that Erasmus admires, not learning in general. Erasmus was neither a philosopher nor a theologian, which is to say that neither Augustine nor Aquinas could be his model. In the most general sense of the word, he was a literary historian, interested in "text and context," eager to set the historical record straight, concerned to reconstruct the Christian past as it actually was, not as it appeared to be in the distorted theology of medieval Schoolmen. Like Colet, he was constantly concerned to ask who was writing a particular document, whom he was addressing, what he was really saying, and what were the surrounding circumstances that help explain what he said. "I consider this the principal key to understanding scriptural difficulties to inquire into what the person who speaks is thinking about," he wrote.[26] To the serious student of Scripture he said: Learn your languages, study the history and geography of the Hebrew and Roman worlds, soak yourself in the sources, and thus you will recapture the living, breathing Christ, who is a far more compelling figure than the theologized Christ of the Creeds and the Summae. "If the footsteps of Christ be anywhere shown to us, do we Christians not kneel down and adore? Why do we not rather venerate the living and breathing picture of him in these books?" [27] Only thus can we grasp the fact that God became *man*. "We read repeatedly that he pitied the crowd, as in Matthew 20; in Mark 3, that he was angry, and sorrowful; in Mark 8, that he groaned in spirit; in John 12, that he was deeply disturbed in spirit before his passion, and that his anguish in the garden was such

---

[26] Note to I Corinthians 7:42, *Opera, LB*, VI, 701B. Cf. W. Schwarz, *op. cit.*, p. 153.

[27] Paraclesis, *Opera, LB*, V, 144C. This is an echo of Colet. See also Seebohm, *op. cit.*, pp. 204–205, 280; and Huizinga, *Erasmus*, p. 112.

that his sweat was like drops of blood; that he thirsted on
the cross, which was what usually happened during this sort
of execution; that he wept as he contemplated the city of
Jerusalem; that he wept and was moved at the grave of
Lazarus." [28] As a device of Christian piety, there was nothing particularly new about this kind of approach, as readers
of *The Imitation of Christ* (or of Loyola's *Spiritual Exer-
cises*) will recognize. But in Erasmus it was closely allied to
an historical criticism which stemmed from the Revival of
Learning. It reflected the Brethren of the Common Life,
but it also reflected Colet and, above all, Valla.

Erasmus had absorbed Valla's historical perspective, his
sense of the historical discontinuity between pagan antiquity
and the Christian era. Something of the classical conception
of history as an ever-recurring cycle still remained in his
consciousness but in most of his critical work it was the
Christian assumption of a straight-line sequence of unique
events that underlay his thought. From Valla he acquired a
sensitivity to anachronism. On one occasion he ridiculed the
absurdity of the practice, common in some humanistic circles, of using Ciceronian words to describe an utterly different modern world: "Wherever I turn my eyes I see all
things changed, I stand before another stage and I behold
a different play, nay, even a different world." The world
of Cicero (or of Paul) can be understood and even in a
sense relived—but only if we recognize that it had its
unique existence, once, in a past now dead. At the same time,
one revival or renewal in history may suggest the possibility
of another. Rome and her learning had lived and died,
Christian faith had succeeded. "As in time past there had
been a development from learning to piety, from classicism
to Christianity, so in time present learning could restore

[28] Ratio seu Methodus compendio parveniendi ad veram theologiam,
Opera, LB, V, 95A.

piety." Deep in Erasmus' consciousness was the conviction that faith depended on erudition, "that the discovery of the significance of the Christian message and the restoration of piety were the products of historical research." [29]

It was characteristic of the age that its men of learning chose a personal guide to conduct them into an understanding of the past, perhaps in half-conscious imitation of Dante and his Virgil. Erasmus' guide was, of course, Jerome. There was an intense and personal quality about his love for Jerome, like Petrarch's affection for Cicero or Colet's for St. Paul. When Erasmus first conceived the idea of editing Jerome's Letters in 1500, he wrote: "I know not what god inflames and directs my heart. I am moved by the piety of that holy man, of all Christians beyond doubt the most learned and most eloquent." [30] Thirteen years later, with the work almost ready to appear in print, the same thought recurs to him: "The work of correcting and commenting upon Jerome interests my mind so warmly, that I feel as if I have been inspired by some god." [31] The Life of Jerome which he wrote as preface to his edition of the Works was an example of his scholarly work at its best, the first serious attempt to disengage the real Jerome from the miracles and legends and tales of impossible asceticism which had clustered round his name.[32] Erasmus defended Jerome against his critics, fought all his hero's battles over again—and thus

---

[29] This paragraph is a summary of the fine essay of MYRON P. GILMORE on Erasmus' sense of history in *Teachers of History: Essays in honor of Laurence Bradford Packard*, Ithaca, 1954, Chap. I, esp. pp. 20, 24, 25. Erasmus' words quoted are from *Opera, LB*, I, 992C ff. Cf. R. McKEON, "Renaissance and Method in Philosophy," *Studies in the History of Ideas*, New York, 1935, III, 93–95.

[30] ALLEN, I, Ep. 141; NICHOLS, I, Ep. 134.

[31] ALLEN, I, Ep. 273; NICHOLS, II, Ep. 265.

[32] See W. K. FERGUSON'S comment in *Erasmi Opuscula*, Hague, 1933, pp. 125–133. The text of the "Vita" follows, pp. 134–190.

defended himself against his own critics eleven centuries later. The preface to his *New Testament* breathed the same spirit as Jerome's preface, and often repeated the self-same arguments. It was Jerome's kind of mind and Jerome's conception of scholarship that Erasmus admired—literate, witty, illumined by knowledge of the original tongues and by historical imagination, unhampered by dogmatism and authoritarianism. Like Jerome, Erasmus worked "tumultuously," "precipitously" (in his own words). Both were slapdash rather than meticulous in the details of scholarship. It was not that they were temperamentally alike, however. Jerome's ferocious asceticism and violent spiritual tensions were utterly alien to Erasmus. Characteristically, he took little stock in Jerome's Vision. He accepted at face value the saint's later insistence that such things are unimportant and that one should not guide his life by them. It seems very unlikely that Erasmus ever had a dream remotely like Jerome's. Yet the important thing is that he felt himself to be Jerome's spiritual descendant, doing for his age what Jerome had done for his: Restoring and purifying the Christian tradition, relating it to classical culture by means of the best critical and linguistic tools that the pagans themselves had developed.[33]

Erasmus had something, however, that Jerome lacked: a sense of the limits of scholarship—and this is our third observation. No one ever worked harder or longer to save the world by scholarship, but no one realized more keenly the limitations of learning as a road to salvation. Nowhere is the scholar more deftly and delightfully caricatured than in the most famous of Erasmus' books, *The Praise of Folly*.

---

[33] On Erasmus and Jerome, see PRESERVED SMITH, *Erasmus*, pp. 189–192; HUIZINGA, *Erasmus*, pp. 6, 13, 18, 90, 201, 204, 211, 214; ALLEN, *Age of Erasmus*, pp. 138, 144, 162; ALLEN, *Erasmus*, pp. 47 ff. On Jerome's Vision, see FERGUSON, *Opuscula*, pp. 176–177, 181–182.

At one point or another Folly praises all the qualities that intellectuals generally lack (and that Erasmus knew he often lacked): spontaneity, unreflecting directness, unpremeditated thought and action. At one point Folly is even allowed to draw a caricature of the author himself. "Let us compare the lot of the wise man and the fool," she says. The wise man is "a man who wore out his whole boyhood and youth in pursuing the learned disciplines. He wasted the pleasantest time of life in unintermitted watchings, cares, and studies ... always frugal, impecunious, sad, and austere; unfair and strict toward himself, morose and unamiable to others; afflicted by pallor, leanness, invalidism, sore eyes, premature age and white hair; dying before his appointed day. . . . What difference does it make when a man of that sort dies? He has never lived." A little later Folly belabors those who "pursue fame by turning out books" for the edification of a few other scholars. "They add, they alter, they blot out something, they put it back in, they do their work over, they recast it, they show it to friends, they keep it for nine years; yet they never satisfy themselves." Having blasted the learned wisdom that is folly, the speaker goes on to talk of the higher folly that is really wisdom. "The Christian religion on the whole seems to have a kinship with some sort of folly, while it has no alliance whatever with wisdom." It is "children, old people, women, and fools" who take most pleasure in religion. "The original founders of religion, admirably laying hold of pure simplicity, were the bitterest foes of literary learning." [34]

These are light-hearted words with serious undertones, the words of a man who takes his calling seriously and himself lightly. It is no easy state of mind to describe, let alone to maintain. "People say to me: How can scholarly

[34] *The Praise of Folly*, trans. HOYT H. HUDSON, Princeton University Press, 1941, pp. 50–51, 73–74, 118. Used by permission.

knowledge facilitate the understanding of Holy Scripture? My answer is: How does ignorance contribute to it?" [35] Just because a man gives himself whole-heartedly to the profession of Christian scholarship, this does not mean he must believe that learning is the whole of life. Nor if he sees the more human and ridiculous side of the intellectual's profession, this need not mean that he has lost faith in his calling. Erasmus' friend, Sir Thomas More, died for the cause of Christian unity under the Roman Papacy, though he knew as a scholar that the papal claims were a historical growth. Some men can live and even die for a cause—and still remember that there is another side to the question and respect those who choose that side. Erasmus knew his calling as a Christian scholar to be serious and important, but he also knew the presumption in it, the presumption that taints all human aspirations and must often amuse a loving God. In a word, he believed that intellectuals are both necessary and ridiculous.

This is the meaning, I think, of Huizinga's remark that "only when humor illuminated Erasmus' mind did it become truly profound." [36] Erasmus' scholarly work is built solidly into the foundations of modern critical study of the Bible and the Fathers, as Allen points out, but it is deep down and out of sight below the ground level.[37] What lives today from his pen are the less serious things he turned aside to do for relaxation: *The Praise of Folly*, the *Julius Excluded from Paradise*, and the *Colloquies*. Perhaps *The Handbook of a Christian Soldier* should also be included in this category of things done by the way, a scholar's *obiter dicta*. These were not exactly "scholarly works." They would not have helped their author's case for promotion at a mod-

---

[35] De Libero Arbitrio, *Opera*, LB, IX, 1219F.

[36] HUIZINGA, *Erasmus*, p. 78.

[37] ALLEN, *Erasmus*, p. 4.

ern university. But they could have been written only by a scholar, and some of their author's deepest insights were revealed in these lighter works with a freedom and pungency impossible in his more serious works. It was possible, for instance, for Erasmus to have written a learned historical essay, following his model Valla, on the enormous contrast between the simply-organized Christian communities of the apostolic age and the powerful, wealthy, highly-organized Roman Church of his own day. But it was infinitely more effective to imagine the warrior Pope, Julius II, turning up at the pearly gates, haughtily demanding admittance as the Vicar of Christ, and being put in his place by the gate-keeper, the fisherman Simon Peter. The dialogue (which Erasmus certainly wrote, although he never acknowledged the fact) is vivid and racy, laced with broad humor and satire, but the stuff of the argument is taken from the author's learning. "If the Church," says Peter, "is the whole company of Christians, bound together by Christ's spirit, then it seems to me that you have subverted the Church...." The Pope's reply is, "I call the Church the cathedrals, the priests, and especially the Court of Rome, which means me, the Head of the Church." [38] A whole volume could not define so well the two major views of the Church which were mingled in the contemporary Church which Erasmus criticized sharply but clung to all his life.

This leads to our last observation about Erasmus as a Christian scholar: he had a sharp sense of the responsibilities of his calling. This meant in the first place that scholarship must always be relevant to life here and now. Scholarship to Erasmus, as to Colet, is a means to an end, never an end in itself. He could never read a line of a Gospel or of St. Jerome without thinking of its relevance to the problems of

---

[38] *Erasmi Opuscula*, ed. W. K. FERGUSON, Hague, 1933, pp. 115–116.

his own society. He read Matthew 23: 27 on whited sepul-
chres, for instance, and remarked in his note on the passage:
"What would Jerome say could he see the Virgin's milk
exhibited for money, with as much honor paid to it as to the
consecrated body of Christ . . . or the portions of the true
cross, enough . . . to freight a large ship?" He hated war
because it was so utterly incompatible with the "Philosophy
of Christ." To restore the Greek text of the Gospels was to
lay bare this "Philosophy," he reasoned, and this was inevitably to indict a society so given to war as his own. And
so with other institutions and practices which Erasmus condemned or deplored. Unfortunately, he was sometimes as
quick to draw a moral lesson from Scripture as the medieval
Schoolmen had been to draw a theological proposition. But
on the whole, in his interpretation of Scripture he kept as
sane a balance between historical understanding and moral
application as anyone of his age.

Scholarly responsibility meant not only the obligation to
relate the results of study to contemporary need but also the
obligation to publish to as wide an audience as possible. This
was something relatively new, as we have seen. In late
medieval society learning was a monopoly of the Church
and scholarship a concern of the very few. A handful of
Schoolmen wrote in technical theological Latin for each
other. The Revival of Classical Learning in Italy was no
more of a popular movement than Scholasticism had been.
True, the Humanists were mostly laymen or secular-minded
clergymen, but they were as Mandarin-like in their attitude
toward learning as the Schoolmen. There was much intellectual snobbery in Quattrocento Humanism. Many Italian
Humanists despised Dante, the poet of the people, and
many Italian patrons would not have a printed book in their
manuscript libraries. We have glimpsed some of this snobbery in Pico della Mirandola's esotericism and intellectual

pride. His friend, Poliziano, the most polished Latinist of his day, once said that he deliberately chose to write in a difficult classical Latin because he was writing "for the erudite, not for the masses." [39]

There was more than a little of the aristocratic Humanist in Erasmus in his dislike of the *canaille*, in his exquisite tastes and his impatience with ignorance. He knew that only the few would ever have the time or leisure to learn Latin, Greek, and Hebrew, as he advised. In defending his *New Testament*, he wrote that it was written "not for the crowds, but for the erudite, and especially for the candidates of theology." But he also remembered that he came of humble origins and had become a scholar in spite of the difficulties. Vying with his aristocratic tastes there was a strong democratic tendency. The beauties of classical literature were not to be monopolized by a few scholars. (His first book to become popular was his collection of *Adages* culled from Greek and Latin literature for general enjoyment and use.) No more were the Gospels and Epistles the private preserve of theologians. In a famous passage of his "Paraclesis" or Introduction to the New Testament, Erasmus wrote: "I utterly disagree with those who do not want the Holy Scriptures to be read by the uneducated in their own language, as though Christ's teaching was so obscure that it could hardly be understood even by a handful of theologians, or as though the strength of the Christian religion consisted in men's ignorance of it. I wish that every little woman would read the Gospel and the Epistles of Paul. And I wish these were translated into each and every language, so that they might be read and understood not only by Scots and Irishmen, but also by Turks and Saracens.

[39] See P. MONNIER, *Le Quattrocento*, Paris, 1900, I, 326 ff.

... I hope the farmer may sing snatches of Scripture at his plough, that the weaver may hum bits of Scripture to the tune of his shuttle, that the traveller may lighten the weariness of his journey with stories from Scripture." [40] No one knew better than Erasmus that "the Bible is a big book" and that to open it to non-scholars was dangerous. But the strength of Christianity does not consist in men's ignorance of it—he could not escape that. The learned have the heavy responsibility of digging out and refining the Christian truth by which the ordinary man is saved. In presenting the Greek text of the New Testament and saying he hoped it would be translated into every vulgar tongue, he said his final word on the relation between the Christian scholar and the ordinary Christian believer: "Only a few can be scholars," he wrote, "but there is no one who cannot be a Christian." [41]

In perhaps the most "Erasmian" words that Erasmus ever wrote, he once said: "The strange and often confused terms [of the Bible], the metaphors and oblique figures of speech, hold so much difficulty that we must often perspire with effort before we understand the meaning. In my opinion it would be best if some men of both piety and learning were assigned the task of distilling from the purest sources of the Evangelists and the Apostles and from the most approved interpreters the essence of the whole philosophy of Christ—as simply as is compatible with scholarship, as briefly as is compatible with clarity." The results would inevitably

---

[40] *Opera, LB*, V, 140C. On the conflict between aristocratic and democratic tendencies in Erasmus, see W. K. FERGUSON, "Renaissance Tendencies in the Religious Thought of Erasmus," *Journal of the History of Ideas*, XV (1954), 507–508; W. SCHWARZ, *op. cit.*, pp. 157–159; and FRITZ CASPARI, *Humanism and the Social Order in Tudor England*, Chicago, 1954, p. 38.

[41] Doctos esse vix paucis contigit: at nulli non licet esse Christianum, Paraclesis, *Opera, LB*, V, 141F.

win men, because "the most effective agent is Christian truth." [42] Here was an almost Jeffersonian conception of leadership by the *aristoi* and of the power of truth. This was Erasmus at his most characteristic and his best. But who in the hard world of 1518 was to select these men of "piety and learning"? Would they prove worthy of their assigned task? Would the anxious Christians of the early sixteenth century wait for the research to be completed? And would they accept the final results as "Christian truth"? Some ten months before Erasmus wrote these words, an obscure Augustinian friar had posted ninety-five Theses on indulgences for debate in the little university town of Wittenberg. This German Professor of Bible who thus suddenly burst on the public view had developed quite a different conception of the Christian scholar and his calling, one more reminiscent of Augustine than of Jerome.

---

[42] To Paul Volz, 14 Aug. 1518, in ALLEN, III, Ep. 858 (pp. 365–366).

CHAPTER IV

Luther

ERASMUS' New Testament came off John Froben's presses at Basel in March 1516. By the following August a copy had reached Martin Luther, one of the younger members of the faculty of theology at the University of Wittenberg. He was engaged in lecturing on St. Paul's Epistle to the Romans and had finished commenting upon the first eight chapters, using the text of the French scholar, Lefèvre d'Etaples. From the ninth chapter on he used Erasmus' text as his basis. Six years later when he came to translate the New Testament into German, it was from Erasmus' Greek that he worked.

In this Luther was typical of a whole generation of scholars who either owed their inspiration to Erasmus or built upon his work. Almost every major religious leader of the next generation was indebted to Erasmus in one way or another: Archbishop Cranmer, Bishop John Fisher, and Sir Thomas More; Ulrich Zwingli, the Reformer of Zürich,

Martin Bucer of Strasbourg, and John Calvin of Geneva; Cardinals Contarini, Sadoleto, and Pole. Italians, Spaniards, Frenchmen, Germans, Poles, and Englishmen were among Erasmus' close readers and followers. What they drew from his scholarship was, of course, not always predictable. Some were outraged. Some were delighted, without being disturbed in any of their basic beliefs. Some were converted to a Christian Humanism. Some were shocked into more radical reforming careers. Thomas Bilney, for instance, experienced the conversion that was the start of his activity as a reformer while reading Erasmus' *New Testament* of 1516, to which he was attracted simply by the report that the new Latin translation was "eloquently done." [1] A reader could take Erasmus in many different ways, but it was impossible to ignore him.

For two years after Luther published his ninety-five Theses to the world on October 31, 1517, most of the European intelligentsia tended to pigeon-hole the young Wittenberg professor as another Erasmian. Six months after the Theses appeared, Martin Bucer wrote a friend his first impressions of Luther: "He agrees with Erasmus in all things but with this difference in his favor, that what Erasmus only insinuates he teaches openly and freely. . . . He has brought it about that at Wittenberg the ordinary textbooks have all been abolished, while the Greeks, and Jerome, Augustine and Paul, are publicly taught." [2] Luther appeared to be merely another Christian Humanist, another scholarly reformer inspired by the Revival of Learning and perhaps by

---

[1] See C. C. BUTTERWORTH, "Erasmus, Bilney and Foxe," *Bulletin of the New York Public Library*, LVII (Dec. 1953), pp. 576–577

[2] PRESERVED SMITH, ed., *Luther's Correspondence*, Philadelphia, Lutheran Publication Society, 1913, I, Ep. 57. Hereafter cited as SMITH. Quotations which follow from this edition are by permission of the Muhlenberg Press.

Erasmus himself to assail ecclesiastical abuses by attacking men's ignorance of the Philosophy of Christ. If this were the whole story, we should not need to devote a chapter to Luther in this study. We could stop with Erasmus and say: Here was the model of a Christian scholar and his calling in the age of the Reformation; there were others, but they were made in his image.

In order to suggest what dimensions of the problem would escape us if we were to do this, we must run quickly over some familiar ground: Luther's feelings about Erasmus. From the very beginning Luther was torn between admiration for Erasmus the editor and reformer, and suspicion of Erasmus the theologian and Christian. Only a few months after he had begun to use Erasmus' *New Testament* he decided that Erasmus had no grasp of Paul's conception of the law, sin, and grace. To read Erasmus' two lengthy notes on Romans 1: 17 is to gain some inkling of what Luther meant. The first begins by noting that the Latin has no word that exactly corresponds to the Greek for "faith." A long disquisition follows on the various shades of meaning the word may have in both Greek and Latin, in all kinds of compounds. The second begins with Valla's observation that the verb "live" should be rendered in the future tense and gives numerous examples to back up the argument. It closes with a brief reflection which would be too theological for Valla's taste but just as surely too superficial for Luther's: " 'By faith': The preposition signifies origin. For life finds its beginning in this, that we submerge our human senses and believe the words of God. This is said in opposition to the philosophers." [3]

---

[3] Luther to Spalatin, 19 Oct. 1516, SMITH, I, Ep. 21; ERASMUS, *Opera, LB*, VI, 562–564. In 1522 Luther remarked, "Grammar only teaches the words which are signs for real things, as, for example, 'The righteous shall live by faith.' Grammar explains the meaning of 'faith,'

Luther could not share Erasmus' enthusiasm for Jerome. "I consider Jerome as much inferior to Augustine as Erasmus thinks he is superior," he wrote. Jerome "saw nothing but the historical sense of the Scriptures," and Luther feared that Erasmus too was popularizing "the literal, that is the killing, sense of Scripture" followed by "almost all the commentators after Augustine." [4] In the spring of 1517 he wrote that his opinion of Erasmus was becoming worse every day. "I fear he does not sufficiently advance the cause of Christ and God's grace . . . , for human considerations weigh with him more than divine. . . . Everyone who knows Greek and Hebrew is not for that reason a wise Christian, seeing that Jerome, with his five languages, did not equal Augustine with his one, although Erasmus thinks him so superior." [5]

After the indulgence controversy began, Luther was careful not to express his feelings about Erasmus publicly for fear of encouraging the philistines and obscurantists who, he felt, were his enemies as well as Erasmus'. Further, he felt the "mediocrity" of his own learning and talents. But his original doubts remained, and the reasons now became more explicit. "There are many things in Erasmus which seem to me far from the knowledge of Christ, if I may speak as a theologian rather than a grammarian; otherwise there is no man more learned or ingenious than he, not even Jerome whom he so much extols." Scholarship is obviously something more than grammar, learning, and ingenuity to Luther. Spalatin had asked him for guidance in studying

---

'righteous,' 'live'—but it is the sign of the highest art to defend these words against cavillers; this does not pertain to grammar but to theology." *Tischreden, WA*, II, no. 2533, a, b, in W. Schwarz, *Principles and Problems of Biblical Translation*, Cambridge University, 1955, p. 210.

[4] Smith, I, Ep. 21.
[5] Luther to Lang, 1 March 1517, Smith, I, Ep. 30.

the Bible, and Luther replied that the first thing to remember was that "the Bible cannot be mastered by study or talent," but only by prayer and inspiration. "You must completely despair of your own industry and ability and rely solely on the influx of the Spirit." In getting the simple story of the Bible in mind, Jerome can be a help. But when it comes to understanding Christ and God's grace, Augustine and Ambrose are better guides than Jerome, who allegorized too much.[6] A year later Luther was still able to write a letter of warm admiration and respect to Erasmus bespeaking his support. "Wherefore, dear Erasmus, learn, if it please you, to know this little brother in Christ also; he is assuredly your very zealous friend, though he otherwise deserves, on account of his ignorance, only to be buried in a corner, unknown even to your sun and climate." [7]

The link between the two men was Philip Melanchthon, the brilliant young scholar whom Luther was instrumental in bringing to Wittenberg in 1518 as Professor of Greek. Melanchthon was devoted to both and for a time he was able to keep the two from an open breach. But after the Diet of Worms, Erasmus' refusal to join the evangelical cause irritated Luther more and more. In 1523 he compared Erasmus to Moses: "He has done what he was called to do; he has brought us from godless studies to a knowledge of the languages; perhaps he will die with Moses in the plains of Moab, for he does not go forward to the better studies—those that pertain to godliness. I greatly wish he would stop commenting on the Holy Scriptures and writing his *Paraphrases*, for he is not equal to this task. . . . He has done enough in showing us the evil; to show us the good and to lead us into the promised land, he is, I see, unable." [8]

---

[6] Luther to Spalatin, 18 Jan. 1518, SMITH, I, Ep. 47.
[7] 19 March 1519, in PRESERVED SMITH, *Erasmus*, New York, Harper, 1923, p. 220.
[8] Luther to Oecolampadius, 20 June 1523, SMITH, II, Ep. 591.

In the spring of 1524 the word reached Luther that Erasmus was preparing to break openly with him. He wrote Erasmus a bitter letter, urging him not to publish his attack and pouring ironic contempt on his cowardice. Luther now spoke of "the mediocrity of God's gift" in Erasmus, and added, "I for one have never wished you to leave your little sphere to join our camp." [9] In 1524 and 1525 the battle was joined with the publication of Erasmus' *Essay on Free Will* and Luther's *Bondage of the Will*. The opening sentences of each book spoke volumes about the attitude of each author to the problem of Christian truth and how it is to be attained. "Among the difficulties of which there is no lack in the Holy Scriptures," Erasmus begins, "there is perhaps no labyrinth more insoluble than the question of free will." He hopes his brief essay against Luther's views will "contribute to the progress of the truth." "I have so little pleasure in dogmatizing," he continues, "that I would rather put myself on the side of the Sceptics, whenever I am allowed to do so by the inviolable authority of Holy Scripture and by the decisions of the Church, to which I always freely submit my judgments, whether I understand the reasons for what she commands or not." [10] In reply Luther begins by quoting this, to him, appalling statement. "Take away assertions and you take away Christianity," he says. "The Holy Spirit is not a Sceptic." Scripture may be obscure in certain *places*, but not in *things* that count. Its meaning is simple, clear, and plain as day to the discerning heart. God himself may be incomprehensible, but not his Word.[11] An acrid exchange of letters followed. Luther's is lost but we have Erasmus'. "Perhaps you are relying on your own con-

---

[9] c. 15 April 1524, SMITH, II, Ep. 620.

[10] ERASMUS, De Libero Arbitrio, *Opera, LB*, IX, 1215D.

[11] LUTHER, *The Bondage of the Will*, trans. HENRY COLE, Grand Rapids, W. B. Eerdmans Publishing Co., 1931, pp. 18–29.

fession that you are a weak sinner, though at other times you demand everything except to be taken for God. . . . I would wish you a better disposition were you not so marvelously well satisfied with the one you have." [12]

Luther's disposition—on the subject of Erasmus at least —did not improve with the years. In his *Table Talk* mention of Erasmus invariably touches off tirades, sometimes blind, sometimes discerning. Erasmus is ambiguous, flippant, an atheist, "bad through and through," "worthy of great hatred." He "thinks that the Christian religion is either a comedy or a tragedy, and that the things therein described never actually happened, but were invented for the purpose of moral training." "With Erasmus it is translation and nothing else. He is never in earnest." "He has injured the Gospel as much as he has advanced the science of grammar. . . . If I were a young man, I would study the Greek tongue till I knew it perfectly, and then bring out another edition" (of the New Testament).[13] By this time Erasmus had already said his last and most famous word about Luther: "I brought it about that Humanism, which among the Italians . . . savored of nothing but pure paganism, began nobly to celebrate Christ. . . . While I was fighting against these monsters [the enemies of learning] a fairly equal battle, lo! suddenly Luther arose and threw the apple of discord into the world." [14]

The issue debated between Erasmus and Luther lies at

---

[12] 11 April 1526, SMITH, II, Ep. 729.
[13] LUTHER, *Tischreden*, in *Werke*, Weimar, 1883 ff., Vol. II, nos. 1597, 2170; V, nos. 5487, 5670. (Hereafter cited as *TR, WA*.) Trans. in *Conversations with Luther*, ed. PRESERVED SMITH and H. P. GALLINGER, Boston, Pilgrim Press, 1915, pp. 108–112. (Hereafter: SMITH and GALLINGER.) Quotations that follow from this work are by permission of the publishers.
[14] Erasmus to Maldonatus, 30 March 1527, ALLEN, VII, Ep. 1805, pp. 15–16, trans. in P. SMITH, *Erasmus*, p. 358.

the very heart of any significant attempt to define the scope
of Christian scholarship. Broadly speaking, as P. S. Allen
remarks, Erasmus was concerned about ignorance, Luther
about sin.[15] One might say, with some exaggeration, that
Erasmus was a scholar turned Christian, Luther a Christian
turned scholar. Luther began by dividing Erasmus into two
halves. He accepted the scholar and rejected the Christian.
Later he put his antagonist together again and rejected both
the scholar and Christian because he felt that Erasmus'
scholarship was vitiated by his misunderstanding of Christianity. At the beginning Luther was grateful at least for
Erasmus' learning and technical erudition in his edition of
the *New Testament*. Years later he was persuaded that the
whole job would have to be done over again. In other words,
he came to believe that a mere grammarian and historian,
concerned to get at the literal meaning and historical context
of a sacred writing, could do positive harm. "Erasmus is a
hollow nut and fouls the mouth." [16] Luther thought of himself as a theologian rather than as a grammarian. If he were
asked to define the function and scope of Christian scholarship, it was clear where he would look for guidance. "Among
writers there is none more worthy of hatred than Jerome,
who had only the name of Christ.... Doctor Staupitz, a
diligent reader of him, used to say, 'I'd very much like to
know how Jerome became a saint.' ... Jerome is a babbler
like Erasmus; he tried to talk big and did not succeed. He
promises the reader something but gives him nothing....
Augustine is a reasoner who will know and not merely imagine, and he teaches something. He is the best theologian who
has written since the apostles." [17] Unless a man be born

---

[15] P. S. ALLEN, *Erasmus*, Oxford, 1934, p. 59.
[16] ALLEN, *Erasmus*, p. 75. Cf. W. SCHWARZ, *Principles and Problems of
Biblical Translation*, pp. 188, 190–192, 196–199.
[17] *TR*, *WA*, III, no. 3011 (cf. I, no. 824); IV, no. 5009. SMITH and
GALLINGER, p. 228.

again, Luther might have said, he can in no way enter into the kingdom of Christian scholarship. Erasmus was an outsider. To him the New Testament was a mere drama, a moral play, not the Word of God proclaiming the Good News of God's saving grace *to him*, to Erasmus. To Luther, Erasmus' greatness as a scholar was limited by his stature as a Christian.

Let us examine this view for a moment without necessarily assuming its validity or its fairness to Erasmus, both of which may be questioned. Luther was asserting the existential factor in the discovery of truth—an assertion which has found strong support at various points throughout Christian history. "How can this uneducated fellow manage to read?" say the Jews in the Fourth Gospel. Jesus replies, "My teaching is not my own but his who sent me; anyone who chooses to do his will, shall understand whether my teaching comes from God or whether I am talking on my own authority" (John 7: 15–17, Moffatt). Augustine would have agreed that commitment is the first step toward knowledge: "Unless you believe, you will not come to know." Pascal, persuading his imaginary listener that he cannot refuse to bet on whether God exists or not, says, "Yes, but you must wager. It is not optional. You are embarked." And in one of his best-known *pensées*, he remarks, "The knowledge of God is very far from the love of him." [18] In a perverse, secularized form, the argument recurs in the contention of Communist intellectuals that all so-called objective scholarship is vitiated by unconscious class bias and by lack of commitment to Marxist belief: he who chooses to do the will of the Party shall understand the truth of the doctrine. Even such an austere discipline as modern physics has reached the conclusion that there is no such thing as pure observation; every observer is also an

---

[18] PASCAL, *Pensées*, Everyman, nos. 233, 280.

actor, inevitably involved in his observation, so that an observation is at the same time an action. From psychology and biology to chemistry and physics, the basic epistemology of science today is perhaps as close to Luther's insistence upon the subjectivity that is an inevitable part of the process of knowing as to Erasmus' painstaking investigation of what Jesus actually thought and said and did, back there, then. Erasmus urged men to revisit first-century Palestine, to go back in time to the birthplace of Christianity—in a sense, their birthplace as Christians—in order to gain a spiritual vantage-point from which the distortions and corruptions of their own day could be viewed in new perspective. But one may visit a birthplace in quite different ways: as a member of the family returning after years away, for instance, with spirit overwhelmed by nostalgic memories of half-forgotten delights; or as a scientific historian gleaning what facts he can from tomb-stones; or as a curious newspaper reporter anxious to pick up a stray anecdote or so about the deceased. Without pressing difficult and dubious analogies any further, let us say simply that Luther was raising a crucial point about Erasmus' scholarship.

To raise an embarrassing point about another scholar, however, is not to prove that one is a scholar oneself. Does Luther belong in this book at all? Was he in any sense a "scholar" as Erasmus, Melanchthon, Cranmer, and Calvin undoubtedly were?

There is a strong case for answering these questions in the affirmative. In its origins the Reformation was a learned movement, an academic affair, a scandal in a university, begun by a professor and spread by his colleagues and students. At the time Luther posted his Theses on indulgences he was a Doctor of Theology and Professor of Bible. Like Colet, he had been lecturing on the Bible to growing numbers of enthusiastic students. He meant to start a gentlemanly academic debate on a point of theology and church practice, as he had done before at Wittenberg on scholasticism. He was motivated by a religious experience which he had undergone some three or four years before while he was in the act of working up lecture-notes on the Bible and attempting to puzzle out St. Paul's real meaning in the first chapter of the Epistle to the Romans. The first converts to his new view of Scripture were his colleagues on the faculty at his university: John Lang, Carlstadt, and Amsdorf in theology, Schurff and Stahelin in law. By the time he nailed his Theses to the door of the Castle Church, he had the support of practically all his colleagues so that his act was, in effect, "the concerted action of the entire institution." [19] The first fruits of his attack on Scholasticism was a curricular revision in the spring of 1518 which provided for adequate instruction in Greek and Hebrew (and led to calling Melanchthon to join the faculty). Within three years student enrollment at Wittenberg had boomed, and apart from his books, Luther's students soon became the chief propagators of his ideas. One of them wrote, "I consider myself fortunate that under God's guidance I have come to a place where, it seems to me, one can learn the Christian religion right; and where the only man who really understands the Bible is living." [20] Pope Leo X thought the whole indulgence controversy a monks' quarrel. It would have been more proper perhaps to call it an academic row. One thing was clear: Luther was no untutored prophet or mystic, no John the Baptist or Mohammed. Ignatius of Loyola had to get his education after his conversion; Luther got his conversion after he received his Doctorate. When he first burst upon the public view, he

[19] E. G. SCHWIEBERT, *Luther and His Times*, Saint Louis, Concordia Publishing House, 1950, p. 300, and 293–302 *passim*.
[20] THOMAS BLAURER, quoted by SCHWIEBERT, *op. cit.*, p. 300.

was a man of learning with more academic status than either Colet or Erasmus or Calvin when the world first heard of them.

As for the mind behind the doctoral degree, there is not much left today of the perverse attempt fifty years ago of Father Denifle to prove that Luther was an ignoramus. Busy Protestant researchers have demonstrated to the satisfaction of most of their Catholic colleagues that Luther had a wide and firm knowledge of the Latin classics, of ecclesiastical history, of scholastic philosophy and theology, and of the Christian Humanists of his own day, in addition to his close acquaintance with the Fathers and his incredible knowledge of the Bible. He acquired a good working knowledge of Greek and Hebrew, though he never had the feel for either that a first-rate linguist like Melanchthon had. He had what we might call today a very high philosophical and theological aptitude, an instinct for historical criticism which was sometimes startlingly good (as evidenced by his prefaces to the various books of the Bible), and an amazing memory. A contemporary who heard him in action during the disputation at Leipzig in 1519 described him as follows: "Luther is extraordinarily learned. Above all, he possesses such an astonishing knowledge of the Bible that he knows almost all of it by heart. He understands enough Greek and Hebrew to be able to give an independent judgment of the value of the translations. He is never at a loss in speaking, such an immense stock of ideas and words does he have at his command." [21] By all the ordinary tests, Luther should qualify as a "scholar."

Yet he never thought of himself as a scholar. He had almost no pride of authorship about his books, kept no list

---

[21] MOSELLANUS, in H. BOEHMER, *Road to Reformation*, Philadelphia, Muhlenberg Press, 1946, p. 288. Cf. H. BOEHMER, *Luther and the Reformation*, New York, 1930, pp. 157–166.

of them, and possessed no copies of many of them in later
life. He took no pride in his style, as the Humanists did,
and he was even more modest about his learning, especially
when he compared it with Melanchthon's. Read the German Bible and Melanchthon's *Commonplaces*, he advised
his students in later years. They might also read his own
commentaries on Romans, Galatians, and Deuteronomy if
they liked, but "there is no better book than this of Melanchthon's except Scripture. He is more concise than I; he
argues and instructs; I am garrulous and rhetorical. If
people follow my advice they will only print my doctrinal
works, though indeed they may read the others [the com-
mentaries] for history to see how things went, for at first it
was not so easy as it now is." [22] To learned men who turned
up their noses at his writings, Luther replied good-natur-
edly that he would leave the salvation of Christendom by
weighty tomes to them so long as they left him free to add
perhaps "a little sermon." [23]

It is hard to imagine Erasmus foreseeing that his commentaries and paraphrases of Scripture would some day
turn out to be of purely historical or biographical interest,
yet Luther had the self-understanding to say this of himself—and it is largely true. His *Liberty of a Christian Man*
is still read by thousands, but his commentaries are of interest mainly to biographers and specialists. All through his
charming and amusing remarks about Melanchthon this
feeling for his own limitations as a scholar peeks through,
alongside his respect for his friend's learning. The two of
them appear in the *Acts of the Apostles*, he once remarked.
Melanchthon is James, brother of the Lord, conservative,
anxious to preserve the law. Luther is Peter, impatient with

[22] *TR, WA*, V, no. 5511; SMITH and GALLINGER, pp. 178–179.
[23] KARL HOLL, *Gesammelte Aufsätze zur Kirchengeschichte*, 6th ed.,
Tübingen, 1932, I, 399–401, 412–413.

the law's burdens. Melanchthon is a worrier, easily disturbed by the great currents of world affairs, while Luther says that great affairs don't bother him because he says to himself, "This is beyond you, you cannot grasp it, so let it go." He therefore frets about little things. Melanchthon is too cautious, too tactful, too apt to see both sides of a question—and he works far too hard. Luther thinks it is better "to speak and hit out like a boy"—and not to work all day Sunday like Melanchthon. And yet he stoutly maintained that the results of Melanchthon's grubbing and grinding were indispensable to the evangelical cause.[24] Whereas Erasmus poked fun at the image of the very scholar in himself, Luther ridiculed the same image by chaffing his younger colleague and devoted friend. Since Luther was never one to spare his own faults, I think the conclusion to be drawn is that he never thought of himself as enough of a scholar to be troubled by the scholar's peculiar sins and failings.

This raises the fundamental question of Luther's consciousness of himself, his calling and mission. If he did not think of himself as primarily a scholar, how did he think of himself? What part if any did scholarship play in his vision of his personal destiny, and how did he come by this vision? It is well to say at the beginning that we cannot expect precise answers to these questions. Not that we lack materials for an answer. Luther was anything but reticent about himself in his later years. The problem is to know how to interpret what he says of himself without doing violence to the historical context. The terms scholar and teacher, prophet and preacher, were not so precise in Luther's day as they seem to us. Luther in his thirties was painfully conscious that he was walking an unknown way,

---

[24] *TR, WA*, I, no. 80; IV, nos. 4577, 4907, 5054, 5091, 5124; SMITH and GALLINGER, pp. 200–204.

following an unnamed profession, sustained only by periods of conviction that God was guiding him in spite of what the highest authorities of Church and State said to the contrary, and shaken in between times by his famous *Anfechtungen*, or attacks of doubt and despair. His self-estimate of one year—or even of one month—was not necessarily that of the next. Erasmus came slowly but surely to a sense of his calling and, as we have seen, it is possible to say fairly precisely what this was. Luther came quite suddenly to an overwhelming sense of God's forgiveness and grace in the revelation to him of the meaning of justification by faith, but it took a long and complex series of external events to bring him to some consciousness of what God meant him to do about it—or rather what God meant to do *through* him. His picture of God's purpose for him never attained the clarity and stability which that of Erasmus did, perhaps because he had such a keen sense of the mystery and freedom of God.

Luther acquired a feeling of personal mission rather late in life. We must remember that until he was past thirty, he never made any important decision which he could feel was really his own. It was others who shaped his life for him until his religious illumination of 1513 or 1514. His decision to study law was apparently his father's. His sudden decision to become a monk was reached in a moment of terror and regretted almost immediately. Certainly he never pictured it later as his own decision, freely made and freely accepted. In the monastery from his novitiate on, as was customary, the essential decisions were made by his spiritual advisers and superiors. They told him when he was ready to profess his vows. They ordered him to prepare himself for the priesthood and set the time for his ordination (in 1507). In the fall of 1508 he was suddenly ordered to leave Erfurt and take the chair of moral philosophy at Wittenberg. After an unhappy year there—he wanted to teach theology not philosophy—he returned to Erfurt to lecture on Lombard's *Sentences*. Finally in September 1511 what proved to be one of the most important decisions of his life was made for him by the wise and kindly Vicar of his Order, Johann Staupitz. Staupitz knew the agony of soul which his young and sensitive Brother had been undergoing. One day he called him in and said to him, "Herr Magister, you must become a doctor and preacher; then you will have something to do." Next day Luther (like Thomas Aquinas before him) had thought up fifteen reasons why he did not feel himself called to be a doctor and preacher. Staupitz would not listen. Did Brother Martin think he was wiser than "the whole congregation and the Fathers"? Luther, near the end of his rope in his spiritual struggles, said he could never stand it for even three months; it would be the death of him. Staupitz tried to laugh him out of his melancholy: "Our Lord God has a lot to do in heaven," he replied. "He needs many clever and wise people to advise him. If you die, you will be received into his council, for he too needs a few doctors." [25] Staupitz guessed that the active life of teaching the Bible to divinity students at Wittenberg would either make Luther or break him, and he hoped it would make him. A year later, on October 19, 1512, at seven o'clock in the morning, Luther received the doctorate, and a week later, also at seven o'clock in the morning (these were serious days), he began his lectures as Professor of Bible at Wittenberg.

Luther became a Doctor and Professor, then, against his will and with no sense of call, if we can believe his later

---

[25] OTTO SCHEEL, *Dokumente zu Luthers Entwicklung*, Tübingen, 1929, nos. 174, 444; see also nos. 230, 485. BOEHMER, *Road to Reformation*, p. 83.

accounts of his feelings—and there is no good reason to doubt them in this instance. In his first few months at Wittenberg his inner distress became even more severe. Perhaps it was during this time that the further conversations with Staupitz took place which he remembered twenty years later. He had been trying to put into words what was wrong with him. "I don't understand," Staupitz said. "Then," Luther remembered, "I thought that I was the only one who had ever experienced these 'spiritual temptations' and I felt like a dead man." One day Staupitz leaned across the table to ask why Luther was so cast down. Didn't he know that such temptations were necessary if anything was ever to come of him? "He thought, of course," Luther remarked, "that I was a scholar, and that if I were not tempted I would become proud." [26] It is not clear what Luther was trying to say here, but it seems likely that part of Staupitz' misunderstanding, as Luther saw it, was his mistaken belief that intellectual pride was at the root of Luther's trouble.

Sometime shortly after this Luther underwent the religious experience that was to change his life. Whatever happened between him and his God in the Tower Room of the Black Monastery at Wittenberg sometime in 1513 or 1514, it was the beginning of his true self-consciousness and sense of calling. He became his own master only when he became mastered by God. From one point of view it was a religious conversion; from another, it was a scholarly discovery. The account which he gave of the experience some thirty years later makes one thing clear: his own spiritual problem and the scholar's problem of understanding St. Paul were inextricably entangled with each other. He was at work on his Lectures on the Psalms, he tells us.

---

[26] Cogitabat enim me esse doctum et nisi tentarer, fore ut superbirem. SCHEEL, *Dokumente*, no. 273. BOEHMER, *Road to Reformation*, p. 103.

I was absorbed by a passionate desire to understand Paul in his Epistle to the Romans. Nothing stood in my way but that one expression, "The justice of God is revealed in the Gospel" (Romans 1: 17). For I hated those words, "the justice of God," because I had been taught to understand them in the scholastic sense as the formal or active justice whereby God, who is righteous, punishes unrighteous sinners. . . . I kept hammering away at those words of Paul, wishing passionately to know what he meant. After I had pondered the problem for days and nights, God took pity on me and I saw the inner connection between the two phrases, "The justice of God is revealed in the Gospel" and "The just shall live by faith." Then I began to understand that this "justice of God" is the righteousness by which the just man lives through the free gift of God, that is to say "by faith"; and that the justice "revealed in the Gospel" is the passive justice of God by which He takes pity on us and justifies us by our faith, as it is written, "The just shall live by faith." Thereupon I felt as if I had been born again and had entered Paradise through wide-open gates. Immediately the whole of Scripture took on a new meaning for me. . . . Whereas the expression "justice of God" had filled me with hate before, I now exalted it as the sweetest of phrases with all the more love. And so this verse of Paul's became in truth the gate to Paradise for me.[27]

A verse which had been a window into Paul's character for Colet and a problem in grammar for Valla and Erasmus had become a key to the whole meaning of Scripture for Luther. It is almost impossible for a naturalistic and relativistic age like our own to grasp what Luther thought had happened. The only analogy that seems helpful is that

---

[27] Preface to Luther's Collected Works, 1545, in *Werke, WA,* LIV, 185–186. Trans. by E. HARRIS HARBISON, in *Great Problems of European Civilization,* ed. K. M. SETTON and H. R. WINKLER. Copyright 1954 by Prentice-Hall, Inc., New York, pp. 252–253. By permission. Cf. BOEHMER, *Road to Reformation,* pp. 114–117; and W. SCHWARZ, *op. cit.,* pp. 210–211.

of a modern scientist searching long and painfully for the answer to some question about nature, to be rewarded suddenly by discovery of the solution as all the pieces miraculously fall into place. Luther like the modern scientist was convinced that there was something *objective* about his discovery (Luther would have said his "recovery") of the truth that a man is saved by his faith in the Father of Jesus Christ, not by his works. The experiment could be performed by anyone else, and if the proper conditions were followed, the same answer would be reached. God's Word, like the book of nature, is *there*, open to anyone to examine. Discovery or recovery of the truth is, to be sure, a gift of grace. But it is not a "revelation" in the sense of a Vision or Voice (Luther was always suspicious of such things). It is a verifiable "insight" (the word is Boehmer's) into what is so.

The truest way, then, to describe the beginning of the Reformation is to say that it originated in *a scholar's insight*, born equally of spiritual struggle and hard intellectual labor. The very character of the sources upon which we depend for our knowledge of Luther's experience illustrates the point. Paul tells us of his experience on the road to Damascus in a letter, and we have another account in *Acts*. Augustine wrote an elaborate spiritual autobiography. In the case of Luther we have his oral reminiscences of many years later but no contemporary letters or autobiography to help us. Our chief reliance is upon his scholarly materials, the books whose margins he filled with his comments and the notes for his lectures on *Psalms*, *Romans*, and *Galatians*, either in his own hand or as written down by his students. Every scrap of this material (some of it discovered only within the past half-century) has been subjected to the kind of minute scrutiny that we usually associate only with New Testament criticism. This scrutiny is still continuing, but we know a great deal about Luther's progress from scholastic modes of thinking to his recapture of Paul's insight into the faith in Christ crucified that is counted as righteousness by a merciful God. We know from these products of a scholar's workshop, in other words, just about where the turning-point in his religious development must have come. And we know this because his scholarly development and his personal search for the assurance of forgiveness were so closely bound up with each other. As Boehmer says, "From the very beginning his struggle for a gracious God was at the same time a struggle for a right understanding of the Bible." [28] The two were always inseparable with him, all his life.

This brings us closer to the heart of Luther's conception of scholarship. Scholarship was never an independent operation of the mind to Luther. During his dark days in the monastery he had acquired a distrust of the unaided human reason and a fear of learning for its own sake that he never lost. Some of this came directly from the Ockhamist critique of reason in which he was so thoroughly trained. Some of it came from his own observation of the abuse of human reason by philosophers and theologians from Aristotle down to the Thomists of his own day. And some of it came from his own intimate experience of the gulf between knowing the way to forgiveness and actually being forgiven. Whatever the sources, Luther saw the demonic possibilities in the intellect while Erasmus saw only its limits as a possible good. Sometimes Luther seems to join the Christian anti-intellectualists, as in his famous outburst on reason as the

---

[28] BOEHMER, *Road to Reformation*, p. 91. "Luther connected the actual text of Holy Writ with the revelation essential for perceiving its real meaning.... Only after study, he maintains, was he granted God's grace." W. SCHWARZ, *op. cit.*, p. 193. See the careful summary of the results of recent scrutiny of Luther's lecture materials in E. G. RUPP, *The Righteousness of God: Luther Studies*, New York, 1953, Part II.

Devil's harlot. But his more considered opinion seems better expressed in his reply to a questioner who asked whether reason was useful to a theologian (the question Aquinas had answered so confidently): "Reason corrupted by the Devil is harmful..., but reason informed by the Spirit is a help in interpreting the Holy Scriptures.... Reason is of service to faith when it is enlightened, since it reflects upon things; but without faith it is of no use." In a lighter vein, he once pointed out the dangers of mixing philosophy and theology. When this happens, he said, men begin to ask Wherefore, Wherefore, Wherefore. "When the Devil came to Eve with the Wherefore, the game was up." [29]

All this means that Luther could never think of himself as a scholar in the way Erasmus did. He never could share the Dutchman's confidence in the saving power of sheer enlightenment, the grace of knowledge. In one of his most brilliant essays, Karl Holl has inquired what Luther thought of himself and his destiny.[30] After 1520 he could not avoid the question, "Who are you? What is your authority?" any more than his Master had been able to. What made it more poignant was that his enemies' questions were echoed in his own inner being. "Must all of our fathers have been fools?" he would ask himself, thinking of the weight of institutional and historical authority against him. "Did the Holy Spirit visit you alone in these last times? Did God allow his people to err all this time?" His answer was generally to say that he had become a reformer against his will in the course of carrying out his "office." But what was his "office"? The very vagueness and

---

[29] *TR, WA*, I, no. 439; V, no. 5534. SMITH and GALLINGER, pp. 115, 124–125.
[30] KARL HOLL, *Gesammelte Aufsätze*, I, 381–419. See also WILHELM PAUCK, *The Heritage of the Reformation*, Glencoe, The Free Press, 1950, Chap. II; and BOEHMER, *Road to Reformation*, pp. 392 ff.

generality of the terms he used at different times to describe it betray his difficulties: "churchman of God's grace," "prophet of the German people," "apostle and evangelist in German lands," "God's unworthy witness." It was only "to spite the devil," he said, that he called himself anything so high-sounding as "prophet." At first he tended to despise his title of Doctor as a "papistical" affair, but after 1524 when he ran into conflict with the unordained Anabaptists, he tended to emphasize the doctorate as the very essence of his office. In the doctorate the Church had imposed upon him the duty of expounding the Scriptures, not only in Wittenberg but to all Christendom, and from this duty all the rest had followed. In the idea of his professorship Luther found what he needed to give his calling historical rootage and institutional significance. As he looked back on it, then, Staupitz' insistence that he take the doctor's degree was providential. However blindly and unwillingly, he had been called to be primarily a doctor and professor of Scripture. "I would be a doctor," he wrote in 1530, "nay, a wonderful doctor; and that name they shall not take from me till the Last Day, that I know for sure." "I would not take all the world's goods for my doctorate," he said in 1532, "for if I did not have this great, heavy responsibility which rests upon me, I would surely be driven to despair and to doubt whether I had not begun this cause without call or command, like a sneak-preacher. But now God and all the world must bear witness that I began publicly, in possession of my doctorate and my preaching office, and that I was led to it by God's grace and help." [31] Luther was not the first or the last to gain

---

[31] *Works of Martin Luther,* ed. C. M. JACOBS *et al.*, Philadelphia, Board of Publication of the United Lutheran Church in America, 1931, V, 19; BOEHMER, *Road to Reformation,* pp. 113–114; HOLL, *op. cit.*, pp. 392–393.

assurance from the belief that his right to speak out rested not only upon his inner call but also upon his D.D.

Luther's conception of his professorship was not that of the nineteenth century. To him the duties of the doctorate included both preaching and teaching, and he never separated the two. His sermons tended to be lectures, and his lectures, sermons. He was always both teacher and preacher, whether in the pulpit or the classroom. In the same way, when he wrote he never distinguished between what we today would call his tracts for the times and his more scholarly works. Letters, sermons, broadsides, devotional tracts, commentaries, and theological tracts flowed from his pen with no label attached to any saying, "This belongs to religious journalism," "This belongs to scholarship," or "This is my *Meisterwerk*." And yet one work stood out from all the rest both in his own estimation and in that of others. On it he worked throughout the last twenty-five years of his life, constantly revising and improving. It was the one thing he was unashamedly proud of. This was his greatest scholarly achievement, his real title to fame as a Christian scholar, his German translation of the Bible.[32]

Looking back on Luther's development, it is easy for us to see that everything in his career up to 1522 could be interpreted as providential training for this supreme task: the years of anguished reading and memorizing of Holy Writ, the conversion experience centered upon new insight into the Word, the iron discipline of learning Greek and Hebrew, the hard-won courage to cut loose from scholastic

---

[32] On the subject in general, see [J.] M. REU, *Luther's German Bible*, Columbus, The Lutheran Book Concern, 1934, particularly Chaps. II, III, VI; JAMES MACKINNON, *Luther and the Reformation*, London, 1925, IV, 273–304; PRESERVED SMITH, *The Life and Letters of Martin Luther*, Boston and New York, 1911, Chap. XXIII; W. SCHWARZ, *op. cit.*, Chap. VI.

exegesis and hew out a fresh line of biblical interpretation
in the early lectures on the Psalms and Epistles, the practice gained by translating some of the Psalms and other
isolated bits of Scripture into German, the feel for direct,
homely speech gained by a sensitive ear and the steady
practice of teaching and preaching in German. Luther did
not quite put it all together in this way, but he knew that
all the obscure twistings and turnings of his life were under
God's providence. "God has led me on as if I were a horse,
putting blinders on me, so that I could not see who came
running up upon me. . . . A good deed rarely issues from
planning wisdom and cleverness; it must all happen in the
vagaries of ignorance." [33] Luther could hardly foresee that
the enforced isolation and physical idleness of the months
at the Wartburg would give him the opportunity to begin
the task for which he was so magnificently prepared. On
December 18, 1521, he wrote John Lang that he would
remain in hiding until Easter. "In the meantime," he said,
"I shall continue to write my Postils and shall translate
the New Testament into German, a thing which my friends
demand and at which I hear that you also are working.
Would that every town had its translator, and that this
book alone might be on the tongues and in the hands, the
eyes, the ears, and the hearts of all men." [34] This is all
we really know about how Luther became a translator,
except that he once remarked years later, "Philip Melanchthon persuaded me to translate the New Testament." [35]
Two weeks before he wrote Lang, he had returned for a few

---

[33] PAUCK, *op. cit.*, p. 16.

[34] SMITH, II, Ep. 518.

[35] Ph. Melanchthon coegit me ad novi testamenti versionem, *Werke, WA*,
XL, 448, 1. 2, in HANS VOLZ, "Melanchthons Anteil an der Lutherbibel,"
Archiv für Reformationsgeschichte, Jahrgang XLV (1954), no. 2, p.
203. On what follows, see this article as a whole (pp. 196–233).

days to Wittenberg. Undoubtedly he saw Melanchthon while he was there, and it is reasonable to suppose that Melanchthon was the chief of those "friends" who apparently urged him to do a translation of the New Testament. Erasmus himself may have had something indirectly to do with the decision since the last sentence quoted of Luther's letter to Lang clearly echoes the "Paraclesis." Whatever the immediate stimulus, Luther seems to have written a first draft in an incredible eleven weeks. He worked from the second edition of Erasmus' Greek—just as he later worked from the best available Hebrew text of the Old Testament—with earlier German translations before him and the Vulgate always in his memory. The result was not only a better vernacular translation of the whole Bible than any of its day from the point of view of faithfulness to the original languages; it was also a literary masterpiece. Much of its accuracy and precision can be traced to the tireless technical assistance of Luther's colleagues, especially Melanchthon. ("A translator should not work alone," he remarked some ten years later, "for the correct and appropriate words do not always occur to one person alone.") [36] But the glory of the German itself belongs to Luther alone.

The Preface to the first edition of the New Testament breathed a spirit quite different from Erasmus' "Paraclesis." Its burden was that the New Testament is a Gospel, not a code of laws—"a good story and report, sounded forth into all the world by the apostles, telling of a true David who strove with sin, death, and devil, and overcame them, and thereby rescued all those who were captive in sin, afflicted with death, and overpowered by the devil.... A poor man, dead in sin and tied for hell, can hear nothing

---

[36] *TR, WA,* I, no. 961.

more comforting than this precious and tender message about Christ, and from the bottom of his heart, he must laugh and be glad over it, if he believes it true. . . . Moses, in his books, drives, compels, threatens, smites and rebukes terribly; for he is a lawgiver and driver . . . [Christ] does not compel us but invites us kindly and says, 'Blessed are the poor, etc.'; and the apostles use the words, 'I exhort,' 'I entreat,' 'I beg.' " [37]

Luther was able to combine three things in his work of translation: (1) a grammatical and historical understanding of the text of a high, though not the highest, quality; (2) a profound spiritual and theological understanding born of his own religious experience; and (3) an unrivalled feel for the possibilities of the German language, backed by an inexhaustible patience in searching out the right word. Translation is a peculiarly difficult art that reveals the inherent problems of Christian scholarship perhaps more vividly than any other variety of scholarly activity. Shall the translator make it his chief aim to bring the reader back to the original in its historical setting by representing the text as faithfully as possible short of literalism? Or shall he bring the original home to his contemporaries by turning its most foreign ideas into phrases perfectly familiar to the reader's everyday experience? The first is the historian's ideal, the second the evangelist's. There is no question where Luther stood if he had to choose. "I try to speak as men do in the market-place," he said. "If I am translating Moses, I want to make him so German that no one would know he was a Jew." [38] Actually Luther de-

---

[37] *Works of Martin Luther*, ed. C. M. JACOBS *et al.*, Philadelphia, Board of Publication of the United Lutheran Church in America, 1932, VI, 440, 442.
[38] *TR, WA*, II, no. 2771a.

manded more freedom in translation than he took in practice, but he was determined to write something the common
man could read. He succeeded so well in Germanizing
the Bible that the reader could scarcely believe the Ten
Commandments and the Beatitudes were not originally
spoken in German. Moses and Christ were brought into
every German hamlet, and men hardly knew they came
from far away in time and place.

There are interesting parallels to Luther's central problem as a translator in the problems that faced the painters
of his age. Luther's younger contemporary Brueghel, for
instance, pictures the Slaughter of the Innocents as a heart-
rending descent of foreign soldiers on a sixteenth-century
Flemish hamlet in winter. He sees the Adoration of the
Magi as the arrival of three wealthy merchants in a crowd
of villagers who are unaware of the shattering significance
of what is taking place in the little hovel in one corner
of the picture. This is something different from the naïve
anachronism characteristic of medieval representation.
Brueghel, like Luther, knows that the Netherlands are
not Judaea and that sixteen centuries lie between. But he
also knows that nothing will bring the pathos and poignancy of the Gospel home more directly to the people than
to paint cruelty and indifference in contemporary garb, to
plant Herod and Christ firmly in sixteenth-century soil.

This suggests both the strength and weakness of Luther's
biblical scholarship in general. When historical and spiritual
understanding compete or conflict, the historical must give
way. To Luther, working on the Psalms in 1513, Christ
was the key to all Scripture: "If I find a nut in the text
with a shell too hard for me to crack, I throw it on the
Rock [of Christ] and I get the sweetest kernel." [39] He

---

[39] REU, *op. cit.*, p. 133, quoting *Werke, WA*, III, 12.

never wavered from this general principle all his life. To make the Psalms more vivid to the reader (like most men of his day he took them to refer to Christ Himself), he changed preterite and future tenses to the present. To be sure, he gave this up when it was pointed out to him that it was grammatically untenable. But he stoutly refused to remove the famous added word in Romans 3:28 where he had written that man is justified "ohne des Gesetzes Werke, *allein* durch den Glauben" (without the works of the law, *only* by faith). His critics stared at it, he said, "like a cow at a new door." But he was writing German, not Latin or Greek, and in German *allein* is used along with the negative to admit one thing and exclude another, as in "I have only eaten and not drunk." To make Paul's meaning "clear and strong" in German, he insisted, the extra word must be there. "We must ask the mother in the home, the children on the street, the common man in the marketplace about this, and look them in the mouth to see how they speak, and afterwards do our translating," he argued. He had a perfectly good case, as a matter of fact. But it was not entirely coincidence that the translation helped make the case for justification by faith alone still "clearer and stronger." [40]

As with grammatical detail, so with historical criticism: theology was the ultimate test. "Let us banish this epistle [of James] from the university," he once said, "for it is worthless. It has no syllable about Christ, not even naming him except once at the beginning. I think it was written by some Jew who had heard of the Christians but not joined them." His published criticisms of James were more moderate, and he later tried to reconcile James with Paul.

---

[40] On Translating, 1530, in *Works of Martin Luther*, ed. C. M. JACOBS, Philadelphia, Board of Publication of the United Lutheran Church in America, 1931, V, 15.

But the ultimate test of genuineness was Luther's spiritual experience, not historical evidence.[41]

Such references to Luther's familiar foibles as a philologist and historian, however, hardly dim his greatness as a translator. In the humanities, unlike the natural sciences, great scholarship is the result not of "objectivity" alone but of a balance between objectivity and sympathy. The ability to stand *outside* the object of study must be balanced by the capacity to get *inside* it in sympathetic imagination. This latter capacity is obviously related to the extent, the depth, and the richness of the scholar's own human experience. A scientist's experience as a husband, a father, a citizen, or a convert to a particular religion, is only indirectly related to his success in understanding the atom. In a literary critic, a historian, or a theologian, however, such experience is directly and intimately related to professional insight. This means that scientists are apt to blossom early, humanists late. To write great criticism, great biography, or great theology, one must be able to stand *within* the situation of other human beings far removed in time and space as well as to stand off *from* them.

Luther knew this. He was persuaded that Christian scholarship must have its foundations in religious experience, no matter how "scientific" the superstructure. "Translating is not an art that everyone can practice," he insisted; "it requires a right pious, faithful, diligent, God-fearing, experienced, practiced heart." [42] "A man becomes a theologian by living, nay rather by dying and being damned, not by understanding, reading, or speculating." [43]

---

[41] *TR, WA,* V, no. 5443. Cf. Reu, *op. cit.,* pp. 170–174, 226; W. Schwarz, *op. cit.,* pp. 171, 179, 181.

[42] *Works of Martin Luther,* ed. Jacobs, V, 19.

[43] Vivendo, immo moriendo et damnando fit theologus, non intelligendo, legendo aut speculando. *Werke, WA,* V, 163, l. 28.

"I did not learn my theology all at once, but I had to search deeper for it, where my temptations carried me." [44] At the close of his life he summed up his faith as a scholar in striking and oft-quoted words: "No one can understand Vergil's *Bucolics* unless he has been a shepherd for five years, nor Vergil's *Georgics* unless he has been a farmer for five years; no one can entirely understand Cicero's *Letters* unless he has taken an important part in the affairs of a large city for twenty years; and no one can think he has sufficiently exhausted the Holy Scriptures unless he has governed congregations with the prophets—Elijah and Elisha, John the Baptist, Christ and the Apostles—for a hundred years." [45]

It is obviously quite impossible to separate Luther the man of faith and Luther the man of learning. Luther the believer wrestling with his recurrent *Anfechtungen* of unbelief, and Luther the scholar groping two, three, or even four weeks for a single word to express something in the Hebrew of Job—these were one and the same person. "You cannot believe how much effort a single verse of a Psalm often costs me," he once wrote.[46] We can assume that the "effort" he described meant both spiritual sweat and honest intellectual labor.

In the history of Christian scholarship, then, Luther belongs with Augustine, not with Jerome, as he saw so clearly himself. Unsystematic as he was, he was still primarily a philosopher and theologian rather than a philologist and historian. Divine illumination and personal inspiration were

---

[44] Ich hab mein theologiam nit auff ein mal gelernt, sonder hab ymmer tieffer und tieffer gubeln mussen, da haben mich meine tentationes hin bracht, quia sine usu non potest disci. *TR, WA*, I, no. 352, l. 12. Cf. RUPP, *op. cit.*, p. 102.

[45] *TR, WA*, V, no. 5468.

[46] Luther to Spalatin, 8 Feb. 1520, *Briefwechsel, WA*, II, 36, l. 29.

the beginning of scholarship to him, theology and chris-
tology the end. But this is not the whole story. He was not
only a theologian. There was something of Erasmus in
him, something of the "Biblical Humanist" in the evangelical theologian. He never imposed personal experience or
official dogmatic teaching upon the text of Scripture in
the way some late medieval mystics and Schoolmen did,
moulding and shaping the meaning of the prophets and
apostles to support either a mystical vision or a scholastic
syllogism. Luther had enormous respect for the text. His
respect for the authority of the Word, his insistence on
getting back to the original sources, his eagerness to restore
the spirit of apostolic Christianity in a corrupt age—all this
was shared by Christian Humanists, as well as by many
Anabaptists. Luther, like Erasmus, was a child of the
Revival of Learning. He absorbed a good deal of the
historical perspective of his age and turned it to his uses.
As a historian, it is true, he would hardly meet the canons
of the modern historical profession any more than Erasmus
would, especially when he confesses that if he wishes to
write, pray, or preach well, then he needs to become angry:
"passion makes books." [47] But he had a keen interest in
history and a profound understanding of its meaning for a
Christian, as recent studies have shown.[48] He was historically-minded in a way medieval theologians were not. He
saw that God reveals and yet at the same time conceals
himself in the historical process. Time was one of the important dimensions of his thinking. Somewhat like Petrarch,
he thought that an earlier age of simplicity and purity

---

[47] *TR, WA*, I, nos. 444, 467; II, no. 2410b. See HOLL, *op. cit.*, I, 410–
411.
[48] See especially HANS LILJE, *Luthers Geschichtsanschauung*, Berlin,
1932; and HEINRICH BORNKAMM, *Luthers geistige Welt*, Lüneburg,
1947, pp. 188–208.

(in this case, Christian) had disappeared, that a Dark Age of superstition and ceremony had followed, and that a new age was dawning. God's hand was working mightily in the events of his own day as it had in those of the past. He never quite worked these ideas out into a philosophy of history, but they gave his whole outlook a dynamism utterly lacking in Aquinas or Abelard.

Luther, then, was first a theologian and a translator, but he was a historically-minded theologian, a historically-conscious translator. He did not stand weeping at the grave of the apostolic age, as Panofsky says the Humanists did at the grave of classical antiquity. He had no sentimental nostalgia for times gone by, as Petrarch and perhaps even Erasmus had. But sometimes he betrayed somewhat parallel emotional attitudes. His affection for St. Paul, like Colet's, had something of the directness and personal quality to it of Petrarch's attachment to Cicero and Erasmus' to Jerome. He named his third son Paul because, he said, St. Paul had given him many a good saying and argument, wherefore he wished to honor him.[49] Whenever he thought of Paul, he imagined him as "a poor, thin little man" like Melanchthon, he said.[50] This would seem to be unmistakably a post-Renaissance attitude, humanistic and Christian at the same time.

As a scholar Luther was almost exclusively concerned with reshaping and purifying the Christian tradition itself. He had little interest in the two other possible aspects of a Christian scholar's calling: relating Christianity to the sur-rounding secular culture, and adapting its thought-forms to scientific discovery. This is true in spite of all that he wrote about war and peace, about government and about economic life. He was never really touched by the Greco-Roman

---

[49] TR, WA, III, no. 2946b.
[50] BOEHMER, Luther and the Reformation, p. 168.

viewpoint, never excited as Erasmus was about the possibility of reviving the best in *both* the classical and Christian traditions. God's accusation of Jerome—"You are a Ciceronian"—never troubled him. But Augustine's cry—"What is wrong with us? The unlearned start up and 'take' heaven, and we, with our learning, but wanting heart, see where we wallow in flesh and blood"—this went to his heart. He was unimpressed by Copernicus' theory because it seemed unimportant. To understand the Word and to give it to the people in their own language—this was his calling. "All I have done is to advance, preach, and teach the Word of God; otherwise I have done nothing ... I have done nothing but let the Word do its work." [51] The Romanist, the Humanist, and the Anabaptist, for various reasons, questioned Luther's objectivity or his inspiration or both. But whether it was merely his word (as they said) or God's Word (as he said), no one questioned that he had made it "clear and strong." This was his achievement as a scholar.

---

[51] *Werke, WA*, X, Part III, pp. 18–19.

Calvin

THE mantle of Luther as leader of European Protestantism fell not upon his friend Melanchthon but upon another scholar of tougher metal, John Calvin of Geneva. Calvin knew Melanchthon but never met Luther. Because he knew no German, he could read only Luther's Latin works, but these he knew well. Luther's influence on Calvin was very large and always warmly acknowledged by the younger man. It was not the direct personal influence of Colet on Erasmus, however. Nor was it like the stimulating but antagonizing influence that Erasmus had on Luther. It was something in between—a long, persistent working of an extraordinary religious mind upon a devoted but critical follower of the next generation whose temperament, training, and social background were worlds removed from his own. Eleven years after Luther's death Calvin was engaged in controversy with one of Luther's followers. "If any vices were mixed with Luther's great virtues," he wrote, "I wish them to remain buried. Certainly reverence and respect for the gifts with which he was endowed keeps me from dwelling upon the vices, whatever they were. But to embrace vices for virtues, that is a foolish and preposterous attitude." [1] These few sentences are characteristic of their writer: his respect for authority, his judiciousness, and not least, his over-riding devotion to the truth.

Almost every facet of scholarship as a Christian calling which we have seen personified in earlier figures is reflected in some way in John Calvin. Like Jerome and Erasmus, Calvin came to sacred studies through an enthusiasm for the pagan classics, and the way he adapted the techniques learned in classical scholarship to the study of Scripture is often reminiscent of both these predecessors. But the way he came to a sense of his vocation—as a result of what he called a "sudden conversion"—was more like the experience of Augustine and Luther. For this reason he was more conscious of their influence on his thinking than of Jerome's and Erasmus'. There are some dozen references to Jerome in the *Institutes*, none of them particularly important, but there are over three hundred to Augustine, many of them buttressing crucial points of the argument. Although neither Erasmus nor Luther is referred to by name in the *Institutes*, the influence of both is there. That of Luther is certainly more pervasive than that of Erasmus, however.[2]

Valla's influence on Calvin cannot be measured by the single reference to him in the *Institutes* as "a man otherwise not much versed in theology" who nevertheless

---

[1] *Johannis Calvini Opera quae supersunt omnia* (*Corpus Reformatorum*), Strasbourg, 1863–1900, IX, 238. (Hereafter, *Opera, CR.*) Cf. FRANÇOIS WENDEL, *Calvin: Sources et évolution de sa pensée religieuse*, Paris, 1950, pp. 97–98.

[2] There is as yet no thorough study. See WENDEL, pp. 94–98.

showed "superior acuteness and judiciousness" on the subject of foreknowledge and predestination. Valla's Latin
style and critical methods, if not his theology, had an important part in forming Calvin's mind.[3] As for Pico della
Mirandola, a recent attempt has been made to prove that
there is a "subterranean dependence" in Calvin's view of
man upon the doctrines of Florentine Neo-Platonism and
upon Pico in particular, a dependence no less real for being
consciously denied.[4] However this may be, Calvin was obviously more directly influenced by the Revival of Learning than was Luther.

Calvin is sometimes called the Thomas Aquinas of Protestantism to suggest that he played somewhat the same role
of synthesizing and systematizing that St. Thomas performed three centuries earlier. At any rate, Aquinas is one
of the very few Schoolmen whom Calvin quotes with
respect in the *Institutes*. Apart from their common interest
in systematizing doctrine, there is little relation between
Calvin and Abelard—unless it be a frivolous one. Abelard,
it will be remembered, like many of his day related scholarship and celibacy closely in his mind and reported without
criticism Heloise's argument that marriage would ruin his
career—which it did. Four centuries later, times had
changed. Many Protestant ministers felt they had to marry
in order to prove their faith. At any rate, Calvin decided
when he was thirty that marriage would be a good thing
for him, before he had anyone in particular in mind. His
object was to find someone "modest, complaisant, unos-

---

[3] Though not so important a part as Breen maintains, I think: QUIRINUS
BREEN, *John Calvin: A Study in French Humanism*, Grand Rapids,
1931, pp. 102–113. WENDEL, p. 94. *Institutes*, III, 23, 6.
[4] ROY W. BATTENHOUSE, "The Doctrine of Man in Calvin and in Renaissance Platonism," *Journal of the History of Ideas*, IX (Oct. 1948),
447–471.

tentatious, thrifty, patient, and likely to be careful of my health," as he put it. After two false starts he found "a grave and honorable woman" who met his prescription. "She was the faithful helper of my ministry," he wrote after her death. "From her I never experienced the slightest hindrance." [5] All of which appears to prove that there is no significant correlation between marriage and success in scholarship as a Christian vocation.

The very catholicity of the influences that played upon him, then, is the first important fact about Calvin as a scholar. He read more widely and was sensitive to more opposing points of view both within and outside the Christian tradition than any of those whom we have considered except Pico. But unlike Pico he was able to find a stable Christian foundation for his erudition, and in this he was more like his favorite Father, St. Augustine. In his conception of his own calling, however, he was unique and unlike any of the others we have discussed.

Calvin was one of those who are so absorbed in a cause that they are reticent about themselves. Only three times in his life did he feel impelled to be autobiographical: once in 1539 in his *Reply to Sadoleto* when he made a veiled reference to his own conversion in describing the arguments of two hypothetical converts to Protestantism: again in 1564 at the end of his life in his last words to the Genevan councillors who visited his sickbed; and most important, in the Preface to his *Commentary on the Psalms* of 1557.[6] This last is so important for our subject that we must look at it closely.

Calvin begins by saying, "If the reading of these commentaries brings as much advantage to the Church of God

---

[5] WILLISTON WALKER, *John Calvin*, New York and London, 1906, pp. 233–236.
[6] In *Opera, CR*, XXXI, 14–36.

as the profit I have gained in writing them, I will have no reason to regret having undertaken this work." The Psalms, he says, are "an anatomy of all parts of the soul." There is no human emotion that is not represented in them as in a mirror—all "the gloom, sadness, fears, doubts, worries, perplexities, yes, all the confused emotions" that agitate the souls of men. From the appalling human weakness revealed in the Psalms, the reader is led on to feel the consolation of prayer and the security of faith. The lesson to be learned is that the infirmities we are ashamed to confess to our fellow men we are free to confess to God, in confidence that our lives are in his hands. This leads Calvin to remark that the conflicts in which God has been pleased to "exercise" him have helped him to understand what was in the minds of the authors of the Psalms, particularly David. He is not to be compared with David, he knows, but he feels they two have something in common. In David's career, in his rise from humble origins to high responsibility, in his patience and zeal, Calvin sees a model set before him by God, as well as a mirror in which he discerns what he describes as "the beginnings of my vocation and the further course of my charge"—that is to say his rise from humble beginnings to the high calling of his ministry in Geneva. His father had destined him for theology but had changed his mind and turned him to the study of law because it was more lucrative. God had other plans for him, however. By a "sudden conversion" God turned him from the papist superstitions in which he seemed to be stuck fast and "reduced his heart to docility." His first taste of true piety so inflamed him with the desire to reap some benefit from his experience, he remembers, that although he stuck at his humanistic studies, he lost his taste for them. Although he was a mere beginner himself, within a year his friends were flocking to him to learn of the Gospel. This was apparently not the "benefit" he wanted nor the opportunity he expected. "Being by nature a bit anti-social and shy," he continues, "I always loved retirement and peace, and I began to look for some hide-out where I could be away from people; but far from gaining my desire, every retreat and hide-away became like a public school to me. In short, although my aim was always to live a private life without being known, God has so taken me about and whirled me around by various vicissitudes that he has never let me rest anywhere, but in spite of my natural inclination, has thrust me into the limelight and made me 'get into the game,' as they say." [7]

The rest of his life Calvin saw as a kind of commentary on this passage. His first attempt to seek seclusion in Basel (January 1535) was disturbed by the news that his fellow Protestants in France were being persecuted and slandered. He felt he had to spring to their defense, as we shall see. A year later he was passing through Geneva, unknown (he thought) to anyone, when the fiery Reformer Farel heard of his presence. "Master William Farel kept me in Geneva not so much by counseling and persuasion as by a terrifying imprecation, as if God had stretched out his hand over me from on high to arrest my steps." When Calvin protested that he had some special studies in hand for which he wished to keep himself free, Farel went to the length of calling on God to curse "the studious quiet and tranquillity" which Calvin was looking for if he refused to help in such a great crisis as the plight of the Gospel in Geneva at that moment. This so frightened and disturbed him, Calvin says, that he stayed. Exile from Geneva three years later came as a relief, and once more he sought seclusion for

[7] *Opera, CR*, XXXI, 22–24.

scholarly work in Basel. This time it was Martin Bucer who routed him out of his retirement by using the same technique Farel had used, but with a new twist. Bucer told him that he was like the prophet Jonah, who thought that by boarding ship he could run away from the Eternal's command to go warn Nineveh of the wrath to come. Once more Calvin was frightened and gave in, this time to become a minister and lecturer in Strasbourg. Not long afterward, regard for his duty to the people of Geneva, an obligation which he considered with "reverence and conscience," led to his return there. It is too long a story, he adds, to tell of his troubles since that return. Like David, he has been besieged not only by Philistines outside his city but also by traitors within. It is these secret enemies at home who rankle most in his mind and help him to understand David when he cries, "Yea, mine own familiar friend, in whom I trusted, which did eat of my bread, hath lifted up his heel against me" (Psalm 41:9). In the welter of false accusations of everything from avarice and luxury to dictatorship and heresy which he had suffered, Calvin concludes that it has been a deep consolation to know that David was similarly afflicted, to find familiar emotional ground in both the despair and the triumph expressed in the Psalms.

Such is Calvin's famous self-portrait, written in his forty-eighth year. All this means first of all, I think, that Calvin, looking back over his life in 1557, thought of himself as a man cut out by nature for one thing—scholarship—and called by God to something quite different—to teaching, preaching, political controversy, religious leadership on an international scale. Naturally "shy," he was called to deal with people rather than with books alone; naturally "timid," he was called to be a kind of general of a crusading army of God; naturally "peaceful" in his instincts, he was constantly aroused to do battle for truth and righteousness by the attacks of enemies and the plight of friends. Here was a man, in other words, who thought of himself as a God-frustrated scholar.

But this cannot be the whole story. The Strasbourg edition of Calvin's works contains fifty-nine stout volumes— quite an output for a frustrated scholar. Not all of this incredible bulk of writing is what we would call scholarship, of course, but a great deal of it is. Do not Calvin's actions speak louder than his words? In spite of what he tells us, was not scholarship always a major part of his vocation as he saw it? Was there really such a gap between his disposition and his calling as he would have us believe? To find an answer to these questions, we must examine the development of his mind and his sense of vocation, using all the available evidence to check his own later interpretation of this development.

The three disciplines that left their mark on Calvin's mind were the scholastic logic which he absorbed at the University of Paris before 1528, the Roman Law which he studied at Orléans and Bourges in the next three years, and the classical studies for which he stole time from his legal studies and to which he devoted himself completely after his father's death in 1531.[8] Calvin as a young man had a way of working strenuously and thoroughly at a body of knowledge without ever quite losing himself in it. Dutifully and conscientiously he mastered the scholastic dialectic, but his emotions were never so involved in his work that he had later to react violently against the whole system, as both Erasmus and Luther did for different reasons.

---

[8] On Calvin's education, see WENDEL, pp. 6–20; BREEN, *op. cit.*, *passim;* and A. M. HUNTER, "The Erudition of John Calvin," *Evangelical Review*, XVIII (1946), 199–208.

When he became a Humanist he ignored or despised
Scholasticism as most good Humanists did, but many of
the mental habits of the Schoolmen remained with him. As
a result there is actually more continuity between Aquinas
and Calvin than between Aquinas and either Erasmus or
Luther. So too with the law, which he dutifully studied at
his father's desire. It influenced his mind but did not
trouble his soul. It seems clear that he kept his emotional
distance in the same way from the Greek and Roman
classics, although this is more debatable. He was undoubtedly more deeply influenced by Humanism than
Luther was. But he never gave his heart to Seneca as
Petrarch did to Cicero or Erasmus to Lucian. Such an
Erasmian thought as the famous "St. Socrates, pray for
me" would never have occurred to the cooler, more objective mind of Calvin in his humanistic phase. In his
Commentary on Seneca's De Clementia of 1532 he admired
and respected his subject, but he also saw his limitations.
In his conversion there was no vision like Jerome's, no
hard choice between pagan and secular studies. The issue,
he tells us quite clearly, was not between Cicero and Christ
but between his loyalty to the Roman Church, its beliefs
and practices, and the Gospel, which at first seemed scan-
dalous and revolutionary to him.[9] His conversion involved
both the mind and the will, but it came to a climax in a
decision of the will and was expressed in the resignation of
his church benefices in the spring of 1534. To be sure, he
tells us that as a result he lost interest in his classical
studies, but the continuity with his humanistic interests was
never really broken. In the later editions of the *Institutes*
references to classical writers increase rather than decrease,
and in 1559 Calvin made a sound classical education the

---

[9] Cf. the Reply to Sadoleto (1539), *Opera, CR,* V, 407 ff.; and the
Preface to the Psalms (1557), *Opera, CR,* XXXI, 22.

foundation of the curriculum in his Genevan Academy. In strange contrast, Erasmus, the Christian Humanist *par excellence*, had turned in his old age to warn against the dangers to Christian faith of a too-enthusiastic classicism, thus foreshadowing the Christian puritanism of a later generation.[10] All this suggests that Calvin preserved closer touch with all the major thought-forms of the past than either Erasmus or Luther, each of whom was more genuinely revolutionary in his own way. He did so because he was more objective in his approach to scholastic, juristic, and humanistic learning, because he could absorb their methods without subscribing to their spirit and swallowing their content, and because he was more catholic in his intellectual tastes.

This is not to say that Calvin's conversion was not a real conversion or that he remained a crypto-Humanist all his life. The preface to the *Commentary on Seneca* published in April 1532 breathes a far different spirit from the Dedicatory Epistle to Francis I written in August 1535 and prefixed to the first edition of the *Institutes*. The first is an elegant, self-assured, and somewhat strained appeal by a young scholar for purely scholarly recognition and acclaim, with hardly a trace of religious concern. The second is a closely-reasoned, but passionate defense of slandered and persecuted co-religionists written by a man imbued with a religious mission greater than himself.[11] Something certainly had happened to this brilliant young writer in the intervening three years.

Between his conversion in 1534 and his final settlement in Geneva in 1541, Calvin gradually discovered what God meant to do with him and through him. From the moment

---

[10] J. Huizinga, *Erasmus*, pp. 172–173.
[11] *Opera, CR*, V, 5–8 (trans. in Quirinus Breen, *op. cit.*, pp. 86–89); and *Opera, CR*, I, 9 ff.

he resigned his benefices in the spring of 1534, he had no
assured source of income, no job, and no prospects. He
was not an ordained priest and never was. His book on
Seneca had caused hardly a ripple of interest, so there
seemed little hope of making a living as a writer. He had
friends, and one of them, Louis du Tillet, he visited for a
time during the summer of 1534 in Angoulême. The house
had a long gallery in which were three or four thousand
volumes, and here the young convert to Protestant doctrine
often buried himself to read.[12] We have glimpses of him
only—writing sermons for neighboring ministers, drawing
strength from a group of like-minded friends, administer-
ing the communion for the first time under a simple order
of service in a cave, with the divine call as his only qualifi-
cation. Sometime in this year 1534 he wrote his first theological tract, an attack on the Anabaptist belief that the soul
slumbers from burial until Judgment Day. The Preface is
"Calvin whole and entire," as Doumergue remarks. Several
good people had urged him to write against the Anabaptists, he says, but his nature was "opposed to all contentions
and debates" and anyway he expected their ravings to
vanish by themselves in time. But their errors had instead
grown and spread. "I know not how I could clear myself
of treason to God's truth if I kept silent," he says. Some
will complain that he is fostering schism and undermining
charity in the Church by writing, but "the crux and beginning of preserving charity," he says, "is that the faith
remain holy and entire among us." [13]

Here was the first reason that Calvin wrote those fifty-

---

[12] FLORIMOND DE RAEMOND, *Histoire de la Naissance, Progrez et Déca-
dence de l'Hérésie de ce Siècle*, Rouen, 1648, pp. 883, 885. Raemond
implies in the next sentence that his source of this information was persons who had seen and known Calvin at this time. See below, note 15.
[13] Preface to Psychopannychia, in *Opera, CR*, V, 169–172.

nine volumes: he could never bear to stand aside and see treason done to God's truth. To preserve the faith holy and entire, he always believed, was more important than to preserve a bland charity. The second reason became evident soon after. This was his passion to organize and systematize, to tie up loose ends and tidy things up in general. Both motives were evident in the writing of the first edition of the *Institutes*.

Erasmus was almost fifty when he published his scholarly *chef-d'oeuvre*, the *Greek New Testament*. Luther was nearly forty when his translation of the New Testament appeared and almost fifty when he finished translating the whole Bible. Calvin was just twenty-six when he wrote his *Institutes of the Christian Religion, containing an almost complete summary of piety and whatever is necessary for all students of piety to know about the doctrine of salvation, a work most worthy to be read and recently published* (as the title-page of 1536 had it). Whether the subtitle was Calvin's or the publisher's we do not know, but this was in truth to be *the* Protestant *Summa*. It was not the first—Melanchthon had shown the way with his *Commonplaces* (1521)—but in its final and much enlarged edition of 1559 it was to be the greatest. Its first appearance at Basel in 1536 demonstrated that the author had discovered his true métier within the broad profession of Christian scholarship—namely that of clarification, organization, and summary of doctrine—at an amazingly early age. His training in dialectic and in law, together with the superb command of both Latin and French which his classical studies had helped to give him, were now harnessed to the evangelical zeal which came from God's "subduing his heart to docility" two years before. The result was one of the masterpieces of Protestant scholarship.

In one of his most glowing passages, Calvin's biographer

Emile Doumergue stops to reflect upon "Calvin's Providential Preparation" for his life's work. Driven out of his native Noyon by the plague, he writes, Calvin in Paris was led to find Cordier, the best Latin teacher in the land, and in Orléans, Wolmar, the best teacher of Greek. The Middle Ages provided him with the Collège de Montaigu to sharpen his dialectical powers, the new age supplied him with the Collège de France to instruct him in languages and the critical techniques of Humanism. The Roman Church exposed her abuses to him and imprisoned him for a time at Noyon to rouse him. The great scholar Lefèvre prolonged his life to one hundred years in order to give the young scholar his blessing at Nérac. Servetus went to Paris to frighten him with his heresy. Finally he was ready. The *Institutes* were the result.[14] This, I fear, is to out-Calvin Calvin himself in deciphering the decrees of Providence, but M. Doumergue's enthusiastic account quite properly emphasizes the remarkable convergence of training, genius, and opportunity which produced the first edition of the *Institutes*.

Precisely how the book grew in its author's mind we are not sure, but recent study has resulted in some interesting conjectures.[15] At some point, probably in 1534 while he was

---

[14] EMILE DOUMERGUE, *Jean Calvin: Les hommes et les choses de son temps*, Lausanne, 1899 ff., I, 513–516

[15] For what follows I am indebted to WALTER G. HARDS' doctoral dissertation, "A Critical Translation and Evaluation of the Nucleus of the 1536 Edition of Calvin's Institutes," Princeton Theological Seminary, 1955 (typed). Hards argues from the fact that there are almost no references to the Fathers in chapters 1, 2, 3, and 6 of the 1536 *Institutes* that Calvin could not have made use of du Tillet's library or of any other while he was in Angoulême. This seems to me utterly out of character. A simpler way to explain the facts is suggested in what follows. See also *Opera, CR*, II, p. xiv; DOUMERGUE, *op. cit.*, IV, 2; PETER BARTH, ed., *J. Calvin Opera Selecta*, I, 31; WALKER, *op. cit.*, p. 137.

in Angoulême, Calvin seems to have conceived the idea of drafting a brief summary of Christian doctrine in the form of a catechism. Possibly some of the homilies he was writing for neighboring ministers formed the nucleus of the work.[16] It may have been written first in French in order to reach the common man, naturally with few scholarly references to the Fathers cluttering the text. The work divided itself into three sections, on the Law, Faith, and Prayer. Possibly another section on Christian Liberty, Ecclesiastical Power, and Political Administration was written at the same time and in the same way. In January 1535 the young author had to flee from France to Basel as French Protestants, among them several of his friends, began to be sent to the stake. In February the French government, in order to mitigate the bad impression made in Germany by the persecution, spread the report that the victims were all Anabaptists and therefore dangerous subversives. This slander added to slaughter was too much for Calvin, who had been living quietly under an assumed name in Basel. He did not see how he could defend himself against the charge of cowardice and disloyalty, he wrote, if he remained silent. The little book originally designed as a confession of faith now became more and more of an apology as two learned sections on the true and false sacraments, replete with scholarly citations, were added. In the end, the earlier catechetical material and the later apologetic sections were put together, all in Latin, to form the six chapters of the first *Institutes*; and in August 1535 Calvin wrote a dedication of the book to King Francis I which made clear its dual purpose. His first aim, he said, was to "lay down some elementary principles by which people who were drawn toward God might find instruction in true piety," particu-

---

[16] This is the suggestion of HENRY BEVERIDGE in his translation of the *Institutes*, Edinburgh, 1845, I, p. vi.

larly his fellow-Protestants in France. But he was also concerned to prove to non-Protestants that the whole evangelical position was being slandered by those who equated it with Anabaptism. The *Institutes* of 1536 were thus addressed to both the persecuted and the persecutors. They were at once a confession and an apology, the work of a scholar with a sensitive social conscience and a keen sense of responsibility.[17]

When Calvin came to look back in 1557 on his motives for writing the *Institutes* over twenty years earlier, he ignored the instructional purpose entirely and mentioned only the apologetic.[18] Actually in successive editions of the *Institutes* the apologetic purpose gradually receded and the instructional purpose became dominant. The Dedication to Francis I and the more purely apologetic chapters remained almost unchanged, while the expository material was enormously expanded. Meanwhile, during the important years of scholarly activity between his expulsion from Geneva in 1538 and his return in 1541, both the systematizing and the apologetic motives continued in rough balance with each other. To clarify the record and to set it straight—these were the two major purposes that shaped Calvin's development as a scholar.

The first of a long line of predominantly apologetic and controversial works appeared in his *Reply to Cardinal Sadoleto* (1539) with its masterly defense of the whole Protestant position. Here, although still only thirty, he wrote as if he felt himself called to speak for European Protestantism

---

[17] Preface to 1536 edition, in *Opera, CR*, I, 9 ff. On the dual purpose of the *Institutes*, see WENDEL, pp. 106–109; FRITZ BÜSSER, *Calvins Urteil über Sich Selbst*, Zürich, 1950, pp. 138–139; and J. T. McNEILL, *The History and Character of Calvinism*, New York, 1954, pp. 124–126.

[18] Preface to Commentary on the Psalms, *Opera, CR*, XXXI, 24.

as a whole. The instructional and organizing urge, on the other hand, was uppermost in his first biblical commentary, that on *Romans* (1539). The ideal commentary, he argued in the dedicatory epistle, is one that is brief and simple, one that conveys the best interpretations of the past to the ordinary reader, one that brings out the religious "usefulness" of the Scripture considered. The reader, he said, should not be disturbed by the fact that interpreters of Holy Writ have not always agreed. "For God has not granted his servants such a great benefit that each of them has been imbued with full, perfect, and absolute knowledge. No doubt He does this partly to humble us, partly to keep us in zeal for brotherly communication. So since we cannot hope in the present life—which otherwise is greatly to be desired—that there be perpetual agreement among us in the understanding of points of Scripture, we must endeavor that when we depart from the opinions of our predecessors we do it not because we are motivated by any lust for novelty, or stirred by malice, or tickled by ambition, but compelled solely by necessity, seeking naught but what is of advantage; however, in religious dogma, in which God especially wishes his peoples' minds to be one, less liberty is to be assumed than in the case of scriptural exegesis. Readers will easily discover zeal for both these objectives in me." [19]

Here was a kind of scholarly confession of faith, a confession which said in effect that the critical and historical approach to Scripture of Erasmus could coexist with the theological approach of Luther. Men might differ on details as historians, but agree on fundamentals as theologians. As a commentator on Scripture—an occupation he loved, and one in which he grew increasingly confident of himself as time went on—Calvin found his own blend between

---

[19] Preface to Commentary on Romans, *Opera, CR*, X, Part I, p. 405.

scholastic, humanistic, and evangelical principles of interpretation. It is the judgment of those qualified to give an
opinion that his theological presuppositions often dictated
his historical interpretations.[20] This is to say that as commentator Calvin belongs more with the theologians, Augustine and Luther, than with the philologists, Jerome and
Erasmus. But we would miss the characteristic mark of his
scholarship entirely if we did not see that he belongs
genuinely to both schools. The Preface to Romans just
quoted, for instance, has as much of Erasmus' respect for
the complexity of Scripture's meaning as it has of Luther's
conviction that the meaning of Scripture is ultimately
simple.

As time went on, the *Institutes* came to be the central
axis round which Calvin's biblical *Commentaries* revolved.
Here in the *Institutes* was the theology upon which Christians could agree, there the various sources or illustrations
of the central doctrines in God's Word. For fuller discussion of doctrinal points, the author of the *Commentaries*
began to refer his readers to the *Institutes*. Calvin was
almost continually engaged in revising and enlarging the
Institutes from the first edition of 1536 until the definitive
edition of 1559, which was completed only by a desperate
and concentrated effort in the midst of illness. The Preface
of August 1559 gives such a clear picture of his own mature
conviction of his calling as a scholar that it is worth quoting
at some length. He begins by mentioning his numerous
revisions of the book. Never until now had he been satisfied
with it. "I should indeed be ill requited for my labor," he
continues, "if I did not content myself with the approba-
tion of God alone, despising equally the foolish and perverse judgments of ignorant men and the calumnies and

[20] See WENDEL, *op. cit.*, pp. 274–275.

detractions of the wicked. For though God hath wholly devoted my mind to study the enlargement of his kingdom and the promotion of general usefulness; and though I have the testimony of my own conscience, of angels, and of God himself that since I undertook the office of a teacher in the Church, I have had no other object in view than to profit the Church by maintaining the pure doctrine of godliness; yet I suppose there is no man more slandered and calumniated than myself. . . . But the devil with all his host is deceived if he think to overwhelm me with vile falsehoods, or to render me more timid, indolent, or dilatory by such indignities. For I trust that God in his infinite goodness will enable me to persevere with patient constancy in the career of his holy calling; of which I afford my pious readers a fresh proof in this edition." [21]

The evidence is overwhelming, in other words, that Calvin considered writing a major part, if not the very heart, of his calling. From his first theological tract to the final edition of the *Institutes*, the conviction grew upon him that he was called to be the public spokesman of Protestantism, to speak out to his co-religionists everywhere, to defend them against their Romanist enemies, to scotch heresy within their ranks, to systematize their beliefs—in general to use his intellectual gifts and his humanistic training in scholarly work which would advance the Kingdom of God. Of course, if Calvin had been asked in 1559 exactly what he would call himself, it is hard to say just how he would have replied. He would not have said that he was a prophet. Protestantism was a going concern when he appeared on the scene. The time was past for prophets. To his mind this was "an extraordinary office" characteristic of

---

[21] *Opera, CR,* II, 1–4; *Institutes,* trans. JOHN ALLEN, Philadelphia, Presbyterian Board of Christian Education, 1936, Vol. I, pp. 17–19. Used by permission.

the earliest age of the Church and the first generation of
the Reformation, an office which had no place in "well-
established Churches." [22] Of the offices which he recognized in settled churches—pastors, teachers, elders, and
deacons—Calvin was something of both the first two. He
was more clear on the difference between a preacher and a
teacher than Luther had been. A teacher concerns himself
exclusively with interpreting the Word whereas a pastor
also supervises discipline, administers the sacraments, and
exhorts the faithful. A pastor's job is primarily local, while
a teacher or doctor is charged with maintaining sound doctrine in the Church at large.[23] (We have seen this idea
before in Luther.) When he first settled at Geneva, Calvin
signed himself "Lecturer in Holy Scripture in the Church
of Geneva," but he was soon called on to preach and
organize as well. He came to Strasbourg from Basel three
years later as pastor of the Church of French exiles, then
was persuaded by Bucer to take on a teaching position as
well. Calvin, then, was both preacher and teacher all his
life as Luther was, but the two offices were far more distinct
in his own mind.

Unlike Luther, Calvin was neither an ordained priest
nor a Doctor of Theology. He could not depend as Luther
did on a traditional office as the foundation of his calling,
although of course he believed that a pastor properly called
by a congregation was more truly a minister of Christ than
a Roman priest. Calvin's call came to him not through the
laying on of hands nor the conferring of a university
degree, but through his conscience, his study of the Word,
the admonitions of his friends, and the challenge of events.
He had a more intense and constant sense of being God's
instrument than Luther. He wavered sometimes between

---

[22] *Institutes*, IV, 3, 4.
[23] *Institutes*, IV, 3, 4; McNeill, *op. cit.*, p. 218.

apparently conflicting calls—for instance, in 1540 when Geneva and Strasbourg were both competing for his services—but he never seems to have had anything like Luther's *Anfechtungen.* The obstacles in his way were not so much internal as external—open enemies and secret traitors, Roman superstition and Anabaptist heresy. His business was not so much with himself as with the Church and the world at large. And this is why writing—the form of communication which in his day reached the widest audience—was so important to him.

Let us try to set down, if we can, the characteristic marks of Calvin as a Christian scholar, as we tried to do in the case of the others we have considered. The first mark is certainly a passion and genius for systematizing, for bringing order into regions of thought and of the spirit where before there was misunderstanding, confusion, or chaos. In his first published work he remarked (quite characteristically) that one thing he missed in Seneca was "an orderly arrangement, which is not the least among the ornaments of speech." No one has ever missed "orderly arrangement" in anything Calvin ever wrote. In fact, if he has an outstanding weakness as a scholar, it is precisely this tendency to impose order upon the unruly and often irrational raw data of history, Scripture, and experience. Actually, many of his closest students today deny that this tendency ever got beyond bounds. Wendel argues persuasively that if Calvin built a system, it was an "open system," not all derived by inexorable logic from some central principle like the sovereignty of God, but faithful to all the paradoxes of biblical thought and Christian experience.[24] But his love for order and system is undeniable. It appears in his doctrine of the Church as well as in his doctrine of God,

---

[24] Wendel, *op. cit.,* pp. 273–274.

where the emphasis upon God's inscrutability and unaccountability is never pushed so far as to be an argument for "absolute and arbitrary power" contrary to all law.[25] There is a care and fastidiousness, a sense of arrangement, in everything Calvin did as a scholar that argues a fundamentally orderly mind. His genius lay not in creation, but in balancing, harmonizing, and formulation.

The second mark of Calvin's scholarship is closely related to the first. This is the balance he maintained between the subjective and the objective. If it can be said that Erasmus was too little involved as an individual suffering sinner in what he wrote about, and that Luther was perhaps too much involved, then Calvin would seem to have struck a remarkable balance between personal concern and the feeling for objectively verifiable truth in his scholarly work. He had enormous respect for what he recognized as fact, about God, man, or nature. He recognized that the Holy Spirit must impress the divine truth upon the individual heart and mind before it can become operative, but he never doubted the objectivity of the truth itself as revealed once and for all by God in Scripture. He thought of his scholarship as simply clarification of what God had actually said in His Word or revealed in events. There was both strength and weakness in this conviction of the objectivity of God and His truth. The strength is evident, for example, in his answer to Sadoleto's invitation to the people of Geneva to think more seriously of their fate in the future life and to return to Rome: "It is not very sound theology to confine a man's thoughts so to himself, and not to set before him, as the prime motive of his existence, zeal to illustrate the glory of God. For we are born first of all for God, and not for ourselves. . . . It is certainly the part of a

---

[25] See, e.g., *Institutes* III, 23, 2.

Christian man to ascend higher than merely to seek and secure the salvation of his own soul." [26] There is certainly psychological health in this extrovert religious attitude, but there is also danger. The danger is evident in such tracts as his *Answer to the Nicodemites,* those faint-hearted Protestants who conformed outwardly to Roman Catholic practices: "There is no question here of their opinion or mine. I show what I find in Scripture. And I do not hasten to come to a conclusion without considering it well more than three times. What is more, since what I say is well-known, no one can contradict it without plainly denying the word of God. For I say nothing by myself, but I speak by the mouth of the master, citing express witnesses to attest my doctrine from one end to the other." [27]

The third mark is the most significant of all. This is Calvin's concern—perhaps the proper word is obsession—with utility. The idea of usefulness runs "like a red thread" through everything Calvin ever wrote, as Fritz Büsser remarks in a recent study of Calvin's judgment of himself.[28] We have already quoted three passages—from the *Institutes* and the Prefaces to *Romans* and to the *Psalms*—which emphasize the "advantage" or "utility," the "profit" or "fruit," to the reader of what follows. Almost everything that Calvin ever wrote reiterated the same idea.[29]

---

[26] *Opera, CR,* V, 391–392; trans. HENRY BEVERIDGE, in *Tracts Relating to the Reformation by John Calvin,* Edinburgh, 1844, I, 33–34.

[27] *Opera, CR,* VI, 602. For a parallel view of Calvin's concern with the epistemological problem of the relation between subjective and objective truth, see CHARLES TRINKAUS, "Renaissance Problems in Calvin's Theology," in *Studies in the Renaissance,* Austin, University of Texas, 1954, I, pp. 61–62.

[28] BÜSSER, *op. cit.,* pp. 132–134.

[29] See particularly the Traité de la Sainte Cène, *Opera, CR,* V, 429–460; Preface to the Old Geneva Bibles, *Opera, CR,* IX, 823–826; and *Institutes,* I, 17 and III, 1, 1.

At the very beginning of his career as a scholar, Calvin remarked that one trouble with Seneca's Stoicism was its indifference: "Human nature is so built that we are more affected by the viewpoint of utility or of pleasure than by these Stoic paradoxes so far removed from ordinary sentiment." [30] A philosophy, like a theology, he thought, must directly imply an ethic. Any work of the mind must be utilizable in ordinary experience, must produce a "profit" of good works (so to speak) when invested in life, must bear "fruit" in piety and charity. "I do not demand at all," Calvin once wrote, "that people agree with me or my opinion or my say-so, except upon condition that they first recognize that what I teach is useful." [31]

It is legitimate to ask, useful to whom? Erasmus addressed his scholarly works to men of learning, hoping (as he said in his Paraclesis) that the results would trickle down to the people by translation. Luther was very diffident about addressing scholars and did his finest work in translating the Bible into the vernacular in order to reach everyone, even the most humble, in his native land. Calvin sensed the importance of both objectives with his usual acumen and sense of balance. The Latin editions of the *Institutes* after the first were addressed to theological students, as if on the assumption that properly educating the clergy is the key to properly educating the laity. But he was not content with this. In 1541 he translated his Latin into such magnificent French that the result became a classic, one of the chief influences in forming the modern French tongue. In the Preface he emphasized his purpose

---

[30] *Opera, CR,* V, 39.

[31] Ie ne demande point qu'on s'arreste à moy ne à mon opinion, n'à mon dire, sinon à telle condition, qu'on ait premierement congneu que ce que j'enseigne est utile. Contre la secte des libertins, *Opera, CR,* VII, 248. Cf. Büsser, *op. cit.,* p. 106.

of providing a key to the reading of Scripture for anyone, saying it was the duty of students of the Bible (like himself) to show the ordinary reader what to look for. He revised his cousin Olivétan's translation of the Bible into French and let his anger blaze out against those who would keep the Scriptures from the people: "What cruelty it is to take away from poor souls their nourishment to feed them with wind, or rather in place of food to give them deadly poison." [32] He seems to have sensed with remarkable intuition that what the scattered Protestant forces of his day needed, particularly in France, was a leader who could capture the minds of the intellectuals without losing the hearts of the people. It was remarkable how successful he was—with one and the same book. Few if any theological works of the sixteenth century had such success as the *Institutes* in satisfying first-rate minds and at the same time stimulating popular piety.[33] Calvin succeeded in writing "usefully" for a wider range of readers than most theologians in his day or ours. He was hardly too optimistic when he wrote in the Preface of 1559: "I think I have given such a comprehensive summary and orderly arrangement of all branches of religion that, with proper attention, no person will find any difficulty in determining what ought to be the principal objects of his research in the Scripture, and to what end he ought to refer anything it contains."

If we ask, useful for what?, the answer is that scholarship was to be serviceable not only for intellectual clarification and for personal piety but for something far larger: the advancement of the Kingdom. Recent students of Calvin have properly emphasized the overwhelmingly *social* character of his thought.[34] Luther's insights were deepest

---

[32] *Opera, CR*, IX, 824.
[33] See W. WALKER, *op. cit.*, pp. 17, 377; and WENDEL, *op. cit.*, p. 275.
[34] Particularly KARLFRIED FRÖHLICH, *Die Reichgottesidee Calvins*, Munich, 1922, and *Gottesreich, Welt, and Kirche bei Calvin*, Munich, 1930.

in the "I-Thou" relationship. Calvin was constantly concerned with "We," "They," "the Church," "the Elect," "the Kingdom." In a very real sense he collectivized the concepts of prayer, sin, grace, and sacrifice. He was concerned, in a way Luther was not, with "communion and communication" of spiritual benefits.[35] This social concern went along with a startlingly dynamic conception of history. Calvin's God was a busy, active, omnipotent Deity, "not such as is imagined by sophists, vain, idle, and almost asleep, but vigilant, efficacious, operative, and engaged in continual action." [36] And so were his Elect who were to build his Kingdom, his army on the march, pushing out from the narrow beachhead already established at Geneva. "When I consider how important this corner of the world is for the spread of God's Kingdom," he once wrote, "I have reason to be concerned about protecting it." [37] The Kingdom would never be fully established until the Last Judgment, but Calvin's writings were full of the dynamic verbs that describe its progress and growth here on earth in history: *"progredi," "crescere," "provehi."* Utility is a thoroughly social and dynamic concept with Calvin.

Finally, why this striking preoccupation with utility? How are we to explain the broad utilitarian streak in Calvin's conception of scholarship? The easiest way is to say that it was simply part of the spirit of the age. The Italian Humanists who soaked themselves in the classics absorbed the strong ethical interests of the Greek and Roman thinkers. Their chief quarrel with Scholasticism was that its fine-spun abstractions were useless for better living in this world. And so imperceptibly the test of truth with many Humanists became its utility, here, now, in this life. In the long conflict in European thought between the

---

[35] McNeill, *op. cit.*, pp. 214–216.
[36] *Institutes* I, 16, 3.
[37] To Bullinger, May 1549. *Opera, CR*, XIII, 268.

philosophers like Aristotle whose aim it was to contemplate truth and the rhetoricians like Isocrates and Cicero whose business it was to present truth in persuasive and useable form, it seemed as if the rhetoricians were winning out.[38] Valla was a typical rhetorician, anxious to be known as "a true orator" who not only knew "how to speak well" but also had "the courage to speak," [39] more interested in persons than in abstract ideas, concerned always about the ethical implications and applications of doctrine. Machiavelli two generations later was no rhetorician, but he showed the same lack of interest in contemplating useless truth. To him the test of policy was results; the aim of study was to find patterns in political behavior whose knowledge could be useful to statesmen.

The theologians were as much a part of this groundswell of thought as the classical scholars and statesmen. Colet, we have seen, was interested not only in what St. Paul said but also in how what he said applied to the Europe of 1500. Erasmus was constantly pointing out how revolutionary the Philosophy of Christ would be if it were really taken seriously. His objections to Scholasticism were those of the earlier Humanists: it was useless for Christian living. Ignatius of Loyola, in drafting the Constitutions of the Society of Jesus in 1550, consistently subordinated theoretical considerations to getting religious results. In 1558, the year before Calvin published the definitive edition of his *Institutes*, Melanchthon wrote a refutation of the argument of Pico della Mirandola that philosophy

---

[38] QUIRINUS BREEN, "The Terms 'Loci Communes' and 'Loci' in Melanchthon," *Church History*, XVI (Dec. 1947), 197–209; and same, "The Subordination of Philosophy to Rhetoric in Melanchthon," *Archiv für Reformationsgeschichte*, Jahrgang XLIII (1952), no. 1, pp. 13–27.
[39] *On the Donation of Constantine*, ed. C. B. COLEMAN, New Haven, Yale University Press, 1922, p. 23.

was superior to rhetoric. Melanchthon subordinated philosophy to rhetoric and argued that wisdom is useless if it is merely enjoyed in contemplation; it must be declared and explained to ordinary people in clear and intelligible terms.[40]

If a man is purely and simply a product of his age, his mind an accurate reflection of its currents of thought, then all this is explanation enough. Calvin absorbed the ethical interests of the ancients early in his career, as his work on Seneca demonstrated. His respect for Valla and his fine feeling for both the Latin and French languages suggest his high regard for rhetoric. The fact that his "sudden conversion" issued in a moral act—the resignation of his benefices—is proof that his insistence upon the "profit" or "use" of doctrine was no empty theory with him. But the uneasy suspicion remains that there was something more to it than this, something more personal and peculiar to Calvin. Pico was exposed to this same utilitarian current but stoutly defended the scholastic point of view. Luther was relatively uninfluenced by the same current, and many monks and mystics were utterly untouched by it. Why was *Calvin* such a utilitarian in his idea of scholarship?

The clue to an answer lies, I believe, in that famous account of himself which has already been quoted. In the Preface to his *Commentary on the Psalms*, Calvin betrayed an interesting and significant sense of guilt. All his natural inclinations ran toward study and writing, he said in effect. Left to himself, he would have retired from society, surrounded himself with books, and become the pure scholar that he seemed cut out to be. But to Calvin as to Luther, faith is a busy, active thing. It changes society and builds the Kingdom. Faith must result in action—such as resign-

---

[40] Breen in *Archiv für Reformationsgeschichte*, XLIII, p. 17.

ing one's benefices in a corrupt Church, or accepting the clear call of God to preach or teach. And so Calvin felt guilty about his love for learning, as many a Christian scholar had before him—and as many a seminary student has since. This is why he was so stirred and terrified by Farel and Bucer when they called down the divine curse on him if he retreated again to his books. Something in him agreed with them, and he obeyed their exhortations as the call of God. But he was still a scholar at heart and throughout his life he kept returning to his study in the midst of a busy and hectic career to read and write and rewrite.

Only one thing could justify this continual yielding to his early zest for scholarship. This was the idea that the products of his pen could be "useful," could bear "fruit" in thousands of readers miles away in space and perhaps years away in time. Scholarship for its own sake, reading and writing for the sheer fun of it, could never be justified. But if Calvin could keep persuading his readers, and himself, that this was a particular sort of scholarship—sensitive to human needs, relevant to social ills, productive of Christian piety, conducive to better understanding of fundamental beliefs, concrete and vital where the older tradition of Christian learning had been abstract and dead—then scholarship could be a Christian vocation of high significance. This was the heart of his conception of scholarship as a Christian calling.

Conclusion

WE began this study with Tertullian's question, "What has Athens to do with Jerusalem, the Academy with the Church?" We conclude it by admitting that there is no single answer to this question upon which all Christians— let alone all non-Christians—would agree. The author has tried to play the historian to the end: to present his subjects in their own terms and to let the reader draw his own conclusions about what Christian scholarship is, what its chief problems are, and how Christian scholars come by a sense of their calling. But John Calvin might well inquire at this point, What is the use of it all? What is the "profit" and "advantage" of such a study? A hundred years ago in the heyday of German scholarship, this would have been considered a highly improper question. Today it does not seem so improper. In fact, it seems a fair and legitimate question to ask of anyone who writes a book on anything. But since the writer is neither philosopher nor theologian, any answers he offers will necessarily be mere historical *obiter dicta*—to be discounted by all academic readers who still feel that "usefulness" is something to be carefully excluded from all true scholarship.

The question implicit in much that has gone before is whether a Christian can be a "scholar"—that is, a man devoted to books, to reading and writing, to critical analysis or philosophical interpretation, a person addicted to the egotism that seems almost an inseparable part of the pursuit of learning—without spiritual loss. In later centuries, but hardly before the Reformation, the converse of this question would be asked: whether a scholar could be a Christian, without loss of scientific objectivity and professional standing. There will be no attempt here to answer either of these questions for the reader. The plain facts are, as we have seen, that many a great Christian has felt himself called to be a scholar and that scholarship has played a significant role in the development of Christianity. Learning and devotion *have* joined hands in Christian lives at significant moments in Christian history. These lives and these moments are worth study for their own sake, but also for what they may suggest to our own quite different age, an age that defines both scholarship and Christianity more narrowly than did the sixteenth century. Colet and Erasmus, Luther and Calvin, all learned in different ways that "without warmth of commitment scholarship is barren, but without coolness of judgment the results are unreliable" (to borrow a phrase of Roland Bainton's). The lesson is perhaps transferable.

If the age of the Reformation is a fair example, conscious tension between the love of learning and devotion to Christ is a sign of health and vitality in the Christian tradition rather than the reverse. This is not to say that Christianity owes its vitality in any given age to its intellectuals.

The Christian anti-intellectuals certainly have hold of some fraction of the truth. When Christian faith is stripped of everything except what counts, it is clear that what we call the mind has very little to do with it. What Christians believe God did in Jesus Christ, his life, his death, and his resurrection, cannot possibly be comprehended by the human mind. But it has been all too easy down through Christian history for the anti-intellectuals to draw the conclusion that any free use of the mind is therefore dangerous to belief.

In the history of American Christianity, the argument often took a practical turn. A kind of natural suspicion of mere brains has been deep-rooted both in our frontiersmen and our businessmen, and it has often been hard for zealous Christians to justify schools and seminaries, what with so many notorious sinners to be saved and the time so short. Baynard Rush Hall told of the visit of an itinerant preacher to a backwoods community in Indiana in the 1820's. The "meetin'" was held in a neighbor's house with the swine and geese herded for shelter directly beneath the floor. The preacher used a chair for a pulpit, thumping it to emphasize his points. "Thare's some folks, howsomever," he began, glancing at the author and his family, "what thinks preachers must be high larn'd, afore they kin tell sinners as how they must be saved or be 'tarnally lost; but it ain't so I allow—(chair thumped here and answered by a squawk below)—no, no! This apostul of ourn what spoke the text never rubbed his back agin a collige, nor toted about no sheepskins—no, never!—(thump! thump! squawk and two grunts).—Oh, worldlins! How you'd a perished in your sins if the fust preachers had a stay'd till they got sheepskins. No! no! no! I say, give me the sperit." The author remarks that his family always came back from such meetin's "more and more convinced that a learned, talented

167

and pious ministry was, after all, *not* quite so great a curse as many deem it." [1] Only a few years before, a small company of men who thought the same had founded a theological seminary in Princeton, New Jersey. One of them wrote that "the importance of the union of piety and learning in the Holy Ministry is one of those radical principles of ecclesiastical wisdom which the experience of the ages has served more and more to confirm." And so in their "Plan" of the seminary, they stated their belief that "religion without learning, or learning without religion, in the ministers of the Gospel, must ultimately prove injurious to the Church." [2]

The contrast between the mind and "the sperit" has not always been drawn so sharply, but the tension between these two views has always existed in Christian history. It was personified often in the Reformation, notably in the contrast between Thomas Münzer, the Christian revolutionary who relied on the Spirit, and Dr. Martin Luther, who relied on the written Word. Münzer once said, "The man who has not received the living witness of God knows really nothing about God, though he may have swallowed 100,000 Bibles." Luther once remarked that he would not listen to Münzer even though "he had swallowed the Holy Ghost, feathers and all." [3]

Most historians, I suppose, would agree with the

---

[1] BAYNARD RUSH HALL, *The New Purchase*, Princeton University Press, 1916, pp. 170–175. By permission. I owe the reference to MERLE CURTI's presidential address in *American Historical Review*, LX (Jan. 1955), 262.

[2] *Sketch of the Rise, Progress and Present State of the Theological Seminary of the Presbyterian Church in the United States* [by SAMUEL MILLER], Elizabeth-Town, 1817 (pamphlet); *Plan of the Theological Seminary . . .*, adopted by General Assembly, 1811 (pamphlet).

[3] R. H. BAINTON, *Here I Stand*, New York and Nashville, Abingdon-Cokesbury, 1950, pp. 261, 264.

founders of Princeton Theological Seminary that "religion without learning or learning without religion" has usually proved injurious to the Church. Like every other religion, Christianity has been periodically plagued by its lunatic fringe of fanatics, obscurantists, and purveyors of superstition and fear. There never has been any really effective remedy against these people except the power of the mind, the patient efforts of an educated ministry. And one might argue that an educated ministry in any age is never any stronger than its few real scholars and seminal minds. It is they who carry out the top-level intellectual jobs which in the long run have much to do with determining the quality of the thinking and writing, the preaching and teaching, of any Christian generation. They study to purify the religious tradition itself, to relate it to the surrounding culture, and to take account of scientific discovery. They are never the motive power of Christianity; they are rather the governor on the driving shaft. To change the figure, their work gives the Christian religion its chance to grow in the surrounding culture. They cultivate the soil, prune away dead branches, and engraft fresh stock. God grants the growth.

Scholarship, then, is a legitimate calling of high significance among Christians. This should be especially true among Protestants—heirs as they are of a movement originated by scholars and intellectuals. The particular scholarly problems that confront each succeeding generation of Christians are different, but the fundamental tasks tend to remain the same. The job of getting back to the sources which Colet and Erasmus set themselves, for instance, is of perennial importance in Christianity, but particularly in periods of rapid and disturbing social change like the sixteenth century or our own. Such ages are particularly tempted to lose the historical Jesus in the Christ of mystical experience. Before Albert Schweitzer went on to his fabulous career as doctor, musician, and missionary in the twentieth century, he went "in quest of the historical Jesus"—a quest that is always important if Christianity is not to become a mystery cult divorced from the historical dimension. Between them, archaeology and form-criticism have worked a revolution in our contemporary thinking about Christian origins comparable to the revolution associated with the names of Erasmus and Luther. So long as Christians believe that God became man, the philologist, the archaeologist, and the historian will continue to occupy the important place in Christian scholarship which they first clearly gained at the time of the Reformation.

Other occupations of Christian scholars of four centuries ago also have their analogues today, but there are also unprecedented problems as well. Translation can still be a creative achievement. The Revised Standard Version of the Bible has done much to bring first-century Palestine closer to twentieth-century Anglo-Saxons, and in different ways J. B. Phillips' new version of the Epistles and J. V. Rieu's of the Gospels have done even more. Commentary can still be revolutionary, as Karl Barth's *Commentary on Romans* was in 1918. The unending attempt to reinterpret Christianity in the light of all the deepest insights of contemporary culture continues in theologians like Reinhold Niebuhr and Paul Tillich. These aspirants to the mantle of Calvin and Aquinas, of course, have to wrestle with a problem almost unknown to the Reformers: namely how to take account of a mass of new insights into the nature of man and the universe which stem from a new way of knowing, a highly technical natural science. But the scale of the problem is not so unprecedented as it seems. To adapt Aristotelian logic to Christian uses was perhaps just as difficult an intellectual achievement for Aquinas, to adapt the critical techniques of classical philology just as difficult for Erasmus, as it is today for a Paul Tillich to probe the significance of psychoanalysis for a Christian view of man. The techniques today are far harder to master, but there is nothing new about the problem itself.

One difference between sixteenth-century Europe and twentieth-century America is important. Colet and Erasmus, Luther and Calvin, knew nothing of the institutional separation between great secular universities and independent denominational seminaries which is so typical of the American scene. Our oldest universities were usually the result of religious foundations, but as they became more and more secularized, religious denominations turned to founding their own institutions for the training of priests and ministers. Except, then, for the few cases where a theological school is an integral part of an American university, communities of secular scholars tend to be quite distinct from communities of Christian scholars.

It is hard to see how this can be good for either the university or the seminary in the long run. So far as the universities are concerned, Marjorie Reeves of Oxford has some penetrating comments to make on their situation from her English experience. The two traditional aims of the university have always been to pursue knowledge and to train young men for professional careers in society; in other words, to foster scholarship and teaching. At one time the two aims were bound together, in theory at least, within the context of Christianity. This is no longer true. In the purely secular university the two aims tend to fall apart, research is motivated by nothing much higher than the desire for academic kudos, and teaching becomes mere training for a multitude of specialized vocations. As a result, says Miss Reeves, we are left with "irresponsible learning on the one side, and equally irresponsible technical competence on the other, with disastrous results to our culture." [4] So far as the seminaries are concerned, the typical danger is professional isolation from all the daily, intimate contact with secular thought and scholarship that made the medieval university of Aquinas' day or even Luther's little University of Wittenberg such exciting and fruitful places in which to train future priests and ministers.

Colet and Erasmus, Luther and Calvin, knew nothing of "secular" universities and "denominational" seminaries, although Calvin's Academy at Geneva foreshadowed the later separation. The danger is that our seminaries will become mere ministerial "trade-schools," cut off from all fruitful contact with higher learning in other fields, and that our universities will become purely secular centers of research and vocational training, divorced from all contact with religious scholarship. The solution is not to attempt to restore the medieval university in twentieth-century society. Secular university and denominational seminary can hardly be reunited in a pluralistic society. The only possible solution would seem to be the deliberate development of more fruitful contact between the two sorts of institution through their members. The danger of final separation between sacred and secular learning can only be avoided if more men and women in both seminaries and universities acquire the vision of scholarship as a calling worthy of a Christian, and of Christianity as a commitment worthy of a scholar.

---

[4] *The Christian Scholar*, XXXVII, Supplement (Autumn 1954), 189.

Index